Now That's QUICK SERVICE THAT SELLS!®

The Art of Managing the Sizzle for Quick-Service Restaurants

PENCOM®
INTERNATIONAL
Real World Training Solutions

www.pencominternational.com | 800.247.8514

ISBN: # 1-879239-45-0

PUB-516
5/2004

Written by TJ Schier for Pencom International
Edited by Bill Nelson and Kristen Kent
Cover and interior design by Deborah Henckel

Contents

Introduction

INTRODUCTION

Most restaurant guests have had "average" service experiences or those which go terribly wrong. And the funny thing is, many employees — and even managers — at the time would say they had done a good job, or at least what their company wants. How would they know? They're simply a product of the environment the company and managers have created.

Whether you run a pizza delivery/carryout operation, a quick-service or fast-casual restaurant, time with the guest is a "limited-interactive environment." **Guests expect food quickly and tend to give us a little leeway if we can deliver the basics:**

- O Greet (face-to-face, drive-thru speaker or phone)
- O Take Order
- O Suggestively Sell
- O Make Food
- O Deliver Food
- O Thank

3

These steps provide guidance but allow for little flexibility and personality. After all, shouldn't it be the guests who determine what kind of service they want?

Airlines, for instance, still review how to fasten a seatbelt prior to takeoff. Is there any flier left on the planet who doesn't know how to buckle up? As a very frequent-flier myself, do I like being drawn through the whole evacuation process? I know there are 50 ways to leave your lover but only four ways to get off the airplane. Come on, adapt with the times and add some flair to your service steps.

Your guests today need more than "G.E.D. Service" — Greet, Eat, Delete. When I talk to employees and managers in the habit of delivering uninspired service, they honestly think they're doing what's expected of them.

What's their frame of reference? The experiences they receive when eating out at other quick-serve, fast-casual and pizza operations. Most have not been to a fine-dining establishment or stayed at a five-star hotel to understand the breadth of the gap. They can't deliver great service — *Quick Service That Sells!* — because they have no idea what it looks and sounds like.

If yours is a restaurant churning people through a cookie-cutter experience, you can't expect to survive, let alone thrive. Guests are more savvy and thus more demanding than ever before.

Forget being 1% better at 100 things — it's time to step out. **Be unique, be great and be different. Period.** To out-serve the competition you must out-train them. Crush the competition by providing *the* service experience that can't be found anywhere else. Own your guests by creating loyalty.

Over the past few years, airlines, hotels, websites and other businesses have been customizing services according to guests' needs. Sign up for a frequent-stay program at a leading hotel chain and you can enter personal choices for a welcome beverage and snack, not to mention the type of pillow you want upon arrival. Go online and retail sites make recommendations based on what type of items have been viewed. Gone are the good ol' days of "here or to-go?" or "delivery or carry-out?"

People are asking for what they want, when they want it and how they want it. Early on, who would have thought drive-thru would make up as much as 65% of many quick-service restaurants' sales mix? Full-service restaurants offering to-go? The pool of competitors has grown and you must be fantastic to continue to grow sales and guest counts.

The skeptic in you may be saying: "My guests don't expect fine-dining service. Why should I focus on it?" Deliver the unexpected! You can set yourself apart by delivering the unexpected and out of the ordinary — exactly what guests want.

A full-service meal experience comprises 15 to 25 contact points with guests. In quick service, however, there may be only five to 10. Get these right and score in the eyes of the guests. Less can definitely be more!

Ideas are just the beginning — it's how you execute them that makes all the difference in the world. *Now That's* Quick Service That Sells! will show you how to succeed. Here we go.

Author, TJ Schier

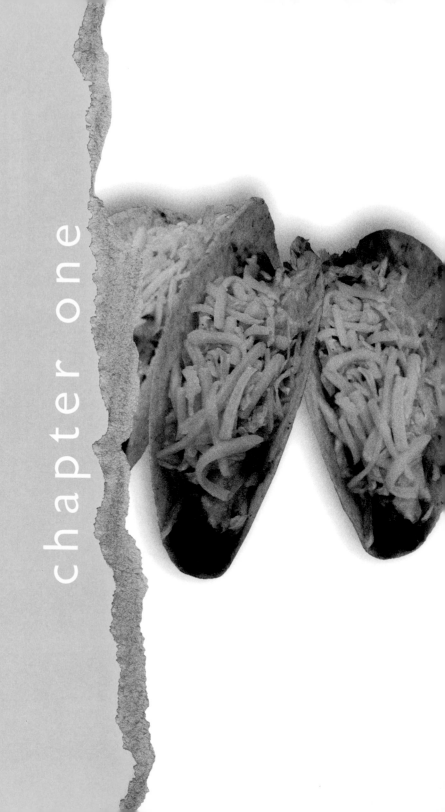

> **Simply the best.** Better than all the rest. Better than anyone. Anyone I ever met.
>
> *Tina Turner — "Simply the Best"*

For more than a dozen years and counting, the best-selling book *Service That Sells!* (Pencom Press) transformed the service guests receive and helped countless restaurants build sales through improved suggestive-selling techniques. It was followed up by **Quick Service That Sells!** which focused on the QSR segment. So why mess with success?

Why write a quick-service sequel?

The marketplace has changed dramatically. Fast-casual concepts, for instance, have given rise to a hybrid experience between quick-serve and full-serve, creating a new line of competitors and diminishing available sales dollars.

With the explosion of fast casual, guests have more control of their dining experience and, in many cases, they even interact with back-of-house crew now given front-of-the-house duties.

Great food at lower prices, combined with the ability to control the duration of experience, is changing the way restaurants do business. Full-service restaurants offering carryout has certainly impacted pizza delivery operations. The new mantra is: "Treat me the way *I* want to be treated, not the way *you* want to treat me." **It's now pronounced** *serve-us,* **not service.**

In some industries, choices are limited. If you need to book a flight, there are few airlines to choose from, depending on the market, and usually few price differences. Loyalty is easy to earn. Almost by default you have to frequent one brand.

With restaurants, however, there is a wide range of options and prices. Loyalty is tougher to earn. For some consumers, your products may not be right, so your restaurant isn't even considered. For other consumers, yours may be just one of countless possibilities. **How do you stand out from the crowd?**

A shipping company's ad sums up the guest focus today: "The most important package is yours." In a restaurant environment, guests don't care how much your crew knows, how good your training program is or how many meals you serve. They care about one thing — their experience. They want it their way on their terms and they're not afraid to tell everyone if it's not right. In fact, there are plenty of websites where guests can post comments for all to read about the unsatisfactory experiences they had.

As guests and competitors raise the bar, it has become necessary to evolve with the times or fade away. ***Now That's*** Quick Service That *Sells!* focuses on what you can do to create high-frequency guests — those who are the most loyal. Numerous books have been written about the link between guest loyalty and long-term profitability. But understanding the link and doing something about it are two different things.

Until the late 1980s, competition was minimal and any form of service brought in business. Competition and restaurant growth exploded in the '90s. **Restaurants that simply provided service were left behind.** Today you have to be "better than expected" versus "pretty good."

Guests have continued to become more selective and demanding. Satisfaction does not drive sales. Shooting for "satisfied" will spell demise. To thrive, restaurants have to aim higher.

Put simply, *Quick Service That Sells!* is delivering hospitality and a customized experience for guests. While they may be on the phone for only two minutes ordering pizza or 90 seconds in the drive thru or 60 seconds with a cashier, the experience needs to be unique. The formula is easy — execution each and every day is not.

The success formula is simple to remember: **S.H.A.Q.**

Speed + Hospitality + Accuracy + Quality

= **Quick Service That Sells!**

Speed. Guests want it quick — that's why they're dining with, or ordering from, your restaurant. They have a need for speed, but not at the expense of other components. Anyone can provide food faster for speed's sake but today's guests demand more.

Hospitality. Not only is it what you say, it's how you say it. Hospitality screams: "We care!" It drives loyalty and frequency. It builds sales by eliminating the competition from guests' minds. It's the emotional attachment you make with guests.

Accuracy. Deliver what guests want to buy, not what the company wants to sell. Guests are demanding and special requests have become the norm. Vegetarian, low carb, no sauce and make it right now!

Quality. Expectations have risen in the eyes of guests. Competitors continue to offer fresher, higher quality food. Guests want value and quality — period.

If you execute effectively in these four areas, sales will increase. It won't happen, however, by itself. Success is in the hands of the manager and crew.

So, what is your role as a manager, owner or franchisee?

○ **Manage the sizzle.** True change starts at the top. Many will read this book, but how many will put it into action? Will you? What's important is talked about constantly. What's important gets resources — time, effort and energy to ensure it happens.

○ **Motivate the crew.** If the desire is to improve the guest experience, enhance the employee experience. If employees don't feel taken care of, they won't take care of guests. Once knowledge has been imparted, the key is to get the crew to put it into action for the benefit of guests as well as sales and profits.

You can work your tail off to please every guest that comes in the door, but you'll be doomed in the long run if you don't fully enlist the help of your crew. Lack of enthusiastic employee involvement within the service-delivery system is the number one reason operations fail to satisfy their guests.

What guests want — **S.H.A.Q.** — comes as no surprise to most quick-service owners, operators and managers. But communicating that knowledge to employees is a whole different enchilada. Time to change!

Not every idea presented will work in every situation. Pick the ones with the greatest chance of success. Use them to enhance strengths and leverage competitive advantages to add distinction to guests' experiences. Make the competition suffer!

> Remember, too, that the term "guests" is better than **"customers."**

Customers shop in retail —
they may or may not buy something.
Guests have already made the decision
to purchase the minute they pull into
the parking lot or call the restaurant.
Therefore, you need to treat them
differently than someone deciding
if they'll purchase something.

Today's guests are savvy, demanding, value-conscious and not prone to loyalty. If so many people aren't even loyal to their spouses or companies, how are they going to be loyal to a restaurant?

You've probably seen those pictures called "photomosaics." From a distance, they appear to be just another picture. Up close, however, you can see hundreds of little photos. The uniqueness is the detail. Otherwise, it's just another picture. In a restaurant, the interaction points between the guests and your crew are the difference-makers. Delivering *Quick Service That Sells!* is all about "sizzle points" — the details in the experience — that wow guests and create a unique visit to your restaurant.

Consider:

While boarding a shuttle at a rental-car business on a hot Raleigh day, a cooler filled with ice-cold bottled waters helped provide a wow on a routine ride back to the airport.

Now That's Quick Service That Sells!

A ho-hum wake-up call becomes a wow:

Guest: "I need a wake-up call at 5 a.m. tomorrow morning."

Front Desk: "That's early! Can I put another one in for 5:15 a.m. just to be sure you get up?"

Guest: "Certainly!"

Now That's Quick Service That Sells!

A quick-serve restaurant doesn't have an order ready when the guest pulls up to the drive-thru window. The driver is asked to park (*aagh!*). A minute or so later a crew member comes up, apologizes and informs the guest that the drink and fry have been upsized at no charge for the inconvenience.

> *Now That's* Quick Service That Sells!

A fast restaurant experience is a series of interactions which, by themselves, don't add up to anything memorable. By providing unique experiences at each point, a picture emerges — a very different one than your competition provides. Sounds easy and it would be if all guests' needs were the same. All guests are not created equal nor are their expectations. Restaurants can't treat everyone the same way — OK — and expect to improve guest frequency. This understanding is a key concept to building a competitive advantage that drives success!

> As far as frequency goes, guests fall into four categories:

1 Cheerleaders

2 Regulars

3 Rotators

4 Ghosts

Cheerleaders. These guests keep you in business. They visit multiple times per week and are your best marketing tool — they spread the good word to others. Make them feel special, know their names and their order, treat them outstanding and they are yours for life. After all, they are driving multiple guests into your restaurant. Cemented to the brand, you wish every guest was as good as these.

Regulars. These guests eat at your restaurant fairly frequently but also visit others. A majority of guests fall into this category. You recognize them but haven't done anything to bond them to the brand. Delivering *Now That's* Quick Service That Sells! will ensure they become cheerleaders and deliver additional sales and profits by spreading the word to other guests. Get out from behind the counter and discover these guests.

Rotators. They enjoy your brand but because of inconsistent experiences they don't frequent you as much as they should or want to. You tend to lose one and gain one, never seeming to get ahead. This group has the potential to be regulars. Find out what their needs are and take care of them.

Ghosts. They don't like your brand. Whether it's the type of food, location or a past bad experience, this group will never visit. Time to forget them.

Bill Cosby once said: "I don't know the key to success, but the key to failure is trying to please everyone." In applying *Quick Service That Sells!* techniques, focus on your high frequency, regulars and rotators, showering them with out-of-the-ordinary hospitality and addressing their individual needs.

Guest frequency stems from building loyalty to a brand — not only in terms of menu, atmosphere and service, but also the employees who put a face on what you're offering. Over time, however, many companies struggle to deliver the basics. Fixated on growing the number of units or hitting earnings per share, they make decisions at the expense of employees and guests to drive short-term gains. Systems and other constraints prohibit even basic delivery of service. The end result?

Guests aren't loyal if they're treated like a number or transaction.

'Good enough' is the enemy of 'better than expected.' "Satisfied" is a far cry from "delighted" or "loyal." Slight improvements in frequency and service levels produce huge gains in sales and profits. It's a phenomenon similar to professional golf. Tiger Woods led the 2002 PGA Tour in money (over $6.9 million) and stroke average (69.0). Drop down the list one shot to the person who averaged 70 per round and he made only $1.4 million. One shot per day! What can managers do to get one more guest in per day, 10 more callers per hour or 10 additional cars through the drive-thru?

With the explosive growth in the number of restaurants and choices, service in many cases has degraded into a series of average experiences. In many towns, guests can eat out every night at a different restaurant for a month (or more) and never eat at the same place twice. With competitors struggling to get food to these guests, there is a tremendous opportunity to set your restaurant apart.

Ask yourself: **What bothers and frustrates guests?** What will they be letting you know about? Why don't they return?

- They're treated like a number ("32, your food is ready." "Next.")
- They're served by insincere employees who don't seem to care or are inadequately trained to handle the business.
- They're ignored or "processed" through the meal.
- They're met by managers who don't want to hear feedback or are unresponsive when it's given. Other managers don't do anything but hold down a position on the line.

Guest service is tough. Why?

- All guests are different.
- Their needs change depending on why they're visiting.

So, how does your restaurant take care of an ever-changing set of needs? The first step is to figure out who the guests are and why they're visiting. When asked for the definition of pornography, a judge once replied: "I may not be able to define pornography, but I know it when I see it."

Outstanding service is the same way — you know it when you see it or experience it.

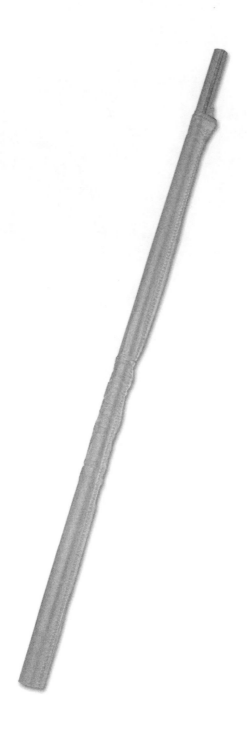

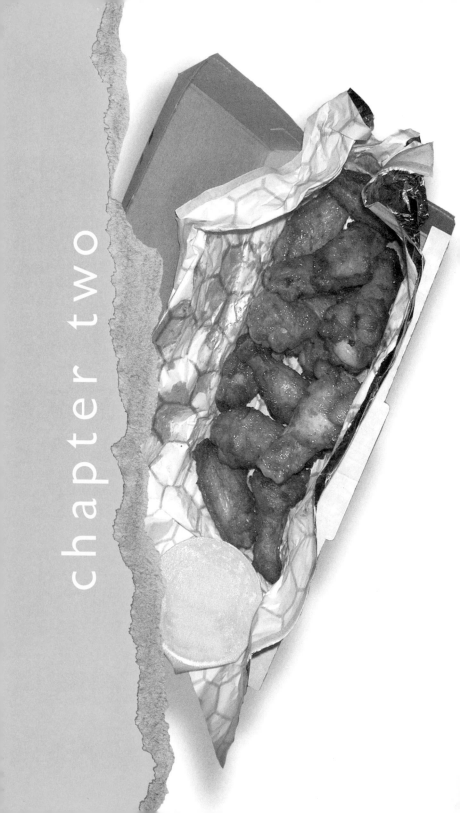

Hospitality

I can't describe it, but
I know it when I see it.

Managers who focus on sales, profits and managing service will struggle to prosper in the long term. It's too easy to be replicated. Competitors will just come along and mimic the tangible — the menu and the prices. Shoot, they may even lower the prices.

It's difficult, on the other hand, to copy the *intangible* — the hospitality your crew delivers on a daily basis. Hospitality drives sales and profits, not the other way around. It's the difference maker, the catapult to greater heights.

The words *service* and *hospitality* tend to be used interchangeably, but they're very different. Service involves steps and tasks to fill a need. A vending machine dispensing a soda is service. Delivering food is service ("Here's your order."). Hospitality is the desire to serve others. It's the flair and personalization of going through the service steps in a unique manner ("One hot delicious chicken combo meal for you, Mr. Smith!"). It's the sizzle that makes you say: "Wow, that place gets it!"

At every contact point guests have with crew, facility and product, they form opinions that sizzle, fizzle or come off neutral. Delivering *Quick Service That Sells!* hospitality ensures those impressions *sizzle*.

Think "three-second sizzle" at each contact point. Encourage your crew members to ask themselves: What can I do right now to delight this guest? Going through the motions and nothing more will make your restaurant just another choice in the marketplace (or one to avoid).

The problem is, **employees and managers often don't know what hospitality looks or sounds like.** It's three-dimensional, not merely words in a book. Tone, body language and actual spoken words determine if it is indeed hospitality or another robotic cashier reciting canned sayings mandated by management. Hospitality is a choice, a state of mind. It's not a program to be implemented and quickly forgotten — it's who you are.

The ideas presented in these pages must be practiced with your crew. Reading words and repeating them to guests without flair, passion or sincerity is actually worse than saying nothing at all. Guests can smell a phony a mile away.

See Appendix A for a Crew Training Handout to help train your staff.

The best way to master the art of delivering hospitality is to experience it firsthand.

There are two alternatives:

send employees to observe restaurants skilled at hospitality

or

use your own hospitable environment as a teaching tool.

If you send employees elsewhere, it's critical to review the visit and relate the experience to their own workplace situation. If you opt for an in-house approach, set up a series of role-plays during which employees can begin to understand the difference between service and hospitality.

For example, greeting guests the proper way instead of chirping: "Next," "Can I take your order?" or "For here or to go?" The three-second sizzle sounds much better: "Welcome! Have you been here before or can I make a few suggestions?"

Guests form opinions within seconds — seconds waiting to be acknowledged, to place an order, to get their food. Eye contact and a warm smile go a long way in helping guests form a positive impression. A "smiling" voice on the phone helps, too. These simple behaviors also minimize dead time and underscore your restaurant's hospitality focus.

Typically, employees today don't have a hospitality skill set when they arrive. They've grown up watching TV personalities and athletes talking smack, being rude, using slang and dressing differently. It's up to managers to teach the right way of doing things.

With the understanding that restaurant concepts have different types of guests and levels of expectations, here are a few words of advice to enlighten the crew:

Avoid terms such as:

"Dudes," "man" or "guys" ("Hey, guys!" when it's a family ordering).

"Cool," "awesome," "kickin," "wicked."

"Whatever," "OK," "No problem (when used instead of "You're welcome")."

"No" or "Can't." Teach employees to offer alternatives: "What we can offer is..." Or: "What I can do for you is..." Or: "Yes, for a slight charge."

"It's our policy." Yeah, and it's the guest's policy not to return when treated in this manner.

To help your crew move from service to hospitality, role-play various interactions. Once again, think three-second sizzle. There isn't time for drawn-out interactions in many cases. You have to wow guests quickly. Consider using a camcorder or "spy-cam" shooting from the point of view of the role-playing guests. This will allow employees to see what they look like through the eyes of those they're serving.

When this is done, typical employee responses heard are: "I didn't know I sounded like that." "Wow! Look how I'm holding my arms, I look mad." "Do I really sound like that?" "The second way sounds much more friendly." And so on. If a picture is worth 1,000 words, video is worth 10,000.

> Let's go to the videotape.

Cashier or Drive-Thru Attendant

The cashier or drive-thru attendant often provides the first and last impression guests have of a restaurant. And those impressions stick, especially if they're unique — positively or negatively. Too frequently, guests are greeted with bland, insincere welcomes.

Be specific with employees or the following will be heard:

Typical Cashier or Drive-Thru Interactions

- "Ready to order?"
- "For here or to go?"
- "Next!"
- "Would you like to try our _____?" (scripted, robotic and mechanical).
- Blank stare at guests until they place the order.
- Head down focused on the POS terminal. Occasional grunt of "OK" to confirm the order.
- No suggestions or inadequate ones: "Anything else?" "Is that all?" "You don't want any dessert, do you?" "Would you like to make that the larger size?" (More on this subject later.)
- No repeat of the order to ensure accuracy.
- Guests hear total, receive change, then are told to step aside.
- The food delivery sequence isn't explained.

Quick Service That Sells! Cashier Interactions

- "Welcome! How is everyone today?"

- "The best deal we have is..."

- "What are you in the mood for?"

- "Have you ever eaten here before?"

- "Hey, kids — are you ready for one of our great kid's meals?"

- Menu guidance is given to first-time guests — most popular items, items the restaurant is known for or the best deals.

- Smiles and eye contact.

- Guest choices are reassured.

- Appropriate suggestions are made in guest-friendly terms. For example, "Would you like to try our large size value meal or save 49 cents and order the regular size?"

- Food delivery sequence is explained if necessary.

- Guests are thanked and told to enjoy their visit!

Now That's Quick Service That Sells!

Typical Body Language

- Frowns, twirling hair, chatting with other employees.
- Leaning on register.
- Arms crossed.
- Waiting for guests to initiate conversation or eye contact.
- Mechanical, robotic and/or standoffish.
- Sloppy, unprofessional appearance.

Quick Service That Sells! Body Language

- Smiles.
- Willingness to approach guests and initiate conversation.
- Eye contact with every guest.
- Glad guests are visiting.
- Professional and polished.

Now That's Quick Service That Sells!

Typical Grooming

- Sloppy uniforms and personal appearance — shirts untucked, dirty or wrinkled, hair, jewelry and shaving standards not followed or very lax.

- No smiles.

- Old, worn out uniform parts.

- No attention to detail about themselves or the uniform.

Quick Service That Sells! Grooming

- Fresh, crisp uniforms.

- Detail to personal appearance — head to toe.

- Smiles!

- 100% compliance of uniform standards and grooming standards.

Now That's Quick Service That Sells!

Each item the guest orders is an opportunity for the cashier, phone rep or drive-thru attendant to "sizzle" the guest (or be just another order-taking drone). Add some flair to make these points sizzle.

Typical Order-Taking Responses

- "OK."
- Silence except for buttons punched on the register.
- "No problem." (Whatever happened to "You're welcome?")
- "You can't make substitutions."
- "You can't get that sandwich as a value meal."
- "I'm not sure what the soup (or special) is today."
- "I don't know if it's good. I've never tried it."
- "I don't think it's that good."
- "Nobody's complained, so it must be OK."
- "Is that it?"
- "Anything else?"
- "NO!" or "You can't."

Quick Service That Sells! Order-Taking Responses

- "Great choice!"
- "It's one of our most popular."
- "Great selection! It's our best seller!"
- "We get a lot of compliments on that."
- "The best deal is to make it a value meal with fries and a soda or side salad and a soda — which would you like?"
- "It goes great with _____."
- "My pleasure."
- "I'd be happy to ..."

*Now **That's** Quick Service That Sells!*

With the advent of fast-casual (or those who have guests move down a food line to order), some food production employees are now in guests' view or may even interact with them as part of the job. Since the cashier in this scenario is typically at the end of the experience, the production employees are handling the welcome and ordering process while the cashier handles the drink order and payment processing. Do these interactions sizzle or fizzle?

Typical Ordering Process

- "What would you like?"
- "What meat? Beans? Cheese? Toppings?"
- "Move down please."
- Processed like a school (or prison) cafeteria line.
- Limited, insincere interaction.

Can guests contain their excitement? What ever happened to friendly chatter and reassurance of the order?

Quick Service That Sells! Ordering Process

- "Welcome to _____! How is everyone tonight?"
  Then one of the following:
- "Everyone ready for an outstanding meal?"
- "I understand it's your first time here. May I make a few suggestions?"
- "Welcome back. Great to see you again!"
- "Great combination on your sandwich/burrito/salad!"
- "That choice is quite popular today!"
- Interaction as the guest moves down the line — have fun!

Now That's Quick Service That Sells!

Once guests have placed their order, food is either delivered or guests are paged to pick up their food. How is the typical food delivery/pickup experience? Pretty bland.

Typical Food Delivery

- Guest treated like a number: "Number 54, your food is ready" or "Here's your order."
- Condiment suggestions non-existent. ("If they want them, they will ask.")
- If guest cannot be located, the paging becomes louder and more sarcastic: "Number 54. Number 54, your food is *still ready. Number 54!*"
- "Number 55, Number 56" and so on.
- "Here is your order. Anything else?"
- Silence as the tray is slid toward the guest at the counter or table.

Quick Service That Sells! Food Delivery

- Order is reviewed with guests as they pick up their food (to ensure accuracy) or described as it is delivered.
- Descriptive words are used when presenting the food or reviewing the order: "Here is your hot, delicious…"
- Guests are asked if they need any specific condiments (or directed to the proper location).
- If food is delivered to the table, any used items such as trays are pre-bused, and drink refills are suggested.
- Guests are thanked for their business: "Thanks again! Don't forget to try the _____ next time!" or "See you tomorrow!"

Now That's Quick Service That Sells!

If guests are dining in the restaurant, do they really expect someone to check on them? Hardly. And exactly the reason it should be done. Managers, get out from behind the counter and set the example for your crew. Begin delivering outstanding hospitality.

Typical Checkback

- Buser walking through the restaurant (head down) clearing tables after guests leave.
- "Done with that?"
- "Is everything OK (or all right)?" (If someone aims low enough chances are they can hit it).
- Guests have to get their own drink refills.
- "Still working on that?"
- Employees walking around with a dirty towel and spray bottle attached to their apron. (That *has* to make the food taste better!)

Quick Service That Sells! Checkback

- Managers and employees interacting with guests.
- Specific questions are asked: "Is your burger/taco/pizza outstanding?" "Aren't those fries great?"
- Drink refills are offered.
- Guests are asked if they have everything they need (utensils, condiments, extra napkins, etc).
- "Are you still enjoying that or may I box it up for you?"
- Managers and employees care — and guests return.

Now That's Quick Service That Sells!

> Employees are on stage, interacting with guests, playing an important role in the visit, yet how long do they get trained? And are they trained on:

How to build rapport with guests.

The menu.

Answering the phone (if applicable).

Interacting with guests to make them feel welcome.

The importance of their role.

Or are they trained in a cursory manner solely focused on what buttons to press on the register? Why let someone interact with nearly every guest without proper training to do so?

To enhance the training of your crew, start with Hospitality 101. What is that? The basics all employees must know:

As guests approach, they enter the Hospitality Zone:

Head up, eye contact and a smile! Yes, this goes for drive-thru, food production employees who interact with guests and phone reps. Guests can hear the smile and confidence in the voice.

As guests near: Personalize the greeting and keep it light and fun!

Be different. Be excellent. The key to delivering hospitality is to read the cues. Deliver the experience guests want, not what you want.

Now That's Quick Service That Sells!

chapter three

Do You Know Who I Am?

"Cut my pizza into six slices; I don't think I can eat eight."

— *Yogi Berra*

Ask employees: "What do we do?" Most responses will be along the lines of: "Serve food." What should be heard? "We allow guests to be pampered and enjoy a dining experience."

Harley Davidson doesn't sell motorcycles; it sells the Harley Experience — allowing people to become an alter-ego. Disney isn't an amusement park, it's an experience. Great shows immerse you and make you feel like part of the action. Is your restaurant an *experience* or just a provider of food and service?

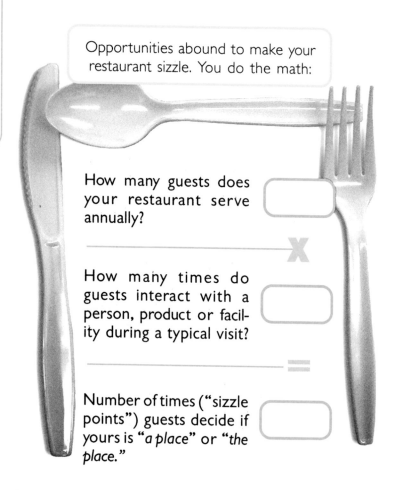

Opportunities abound to make your restaurant sizzle. You do the math:

How many guests does your restaurant serve annually?

X

How many times do guests interact with a person, product or facility during a typical visit?

=

Number of times ("sizzle points") guests decide if yours is *"a place"* or *"the place."*

Everyone's volume and frequency are different, but a typical quick-service restaurant sees more than 200,000 guests per year. On average, guests will interact with a cashier, drive-thru attendant, phone rep, facility (restrooms, beverage bar, landscape, etc.) and product eight to 10 times during the course of a visit. That's more than 1.5 million opportunities to sizzle or fizzle each year!

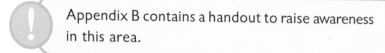

Appendix B contains a handout to raise awareness in this area.

What are the sizzle opportunities in a restaurant? Guests typically interact with crew at the following points:

CASHIER (or food ordering in a cafeteria-style system)

- Initial greeting and welcome.
- Order taking.
- Menu suggestions.
- Food production.
- Payment tendered.

FOOD DELIVERY

- Order paged to be picked up or delivered to table.
- Drink delivery, food order.

CHECKBACK

- Food quality checked on (for dine-in guests only).
- Drink refills.
- Tables pre-bused.

FACILITY

- On-hold message.
- Front entry, doors, drive-thru, parking lot, landscape.
- Speaker quality in drive-thru.
- Menu board.
- Floors.
- Beverage and/or condiment bar.
- Restrooms.
- Music, temperature levels.
- Dining room cleanliness.

PRODUCT

- Beverages.
- Appetizers.
- Value meals.
- Sandwiches, tacos, pizzas.
- Desserts.

Does each point sizzle in your operation? Try this exercise with employees: Have them try to draw their watch. Most look at it numerous times throughout the day, but chances are they can't even remember any details about it. Guests can be the same way — seen but not really known. They're invisible, treated as a series of steps, another "Number 37."

Restaurants try to provide the same steps of service to everyone. Think about the last few times eating out. One time may have been a quick lunch, another you were working on a business deal and needed a little privacy (or wireless internet connection). A family meal. Pizza or wings delivered for the big game or team party.

Where did you go on all those visits? A favorite restaurant, the local lunch spot, the new place that opened in the neighborhood? It's a safe bet your needs were slightly different in each place and on each occasion. What does the perfect experience look like? It depends. Everyone's needs are different.

> Ask employees and managers why guests are ordering from your restaurant. You'll probably hear:

- Great food.
- Good service.
- Atmosphere.
- Friendly employees.
- Location.
- Price.
- Value.
- Unique décor.
- And so on.

Those reasons may help decipher why guests choose one restaurant over another, but they don't tell the whole story. **Warning!** If **guests visit because the restaurant is close to their house or office, a competitor will build one closer.** If they visit because of low prices, a competitor will lower its prices and a winless discounting war will erupt.

> To truly understand what *Quick Service That Sells!* is all about, you have to drill deeper. Why did guests decide to eat out or order delivery/carryout in the first place? The list of reasons forms the foundation for delivering *Quick Service That Sells!*

- Heard about the restaurant and wants to try it.

- No time to cook dinner.

- On the way to a ballgame, kid's event, practice, movie, and need a quick meal.

- Celebrating report cards, doctor visits, lost a tooth, personal success or a milestone.

- Have 45 minutes to eat lunch.

- The kids like the place.

- We like the place and the kids don't mind it.

- Have a group coming over and don't want to cook (delivery/carryout).

- Watching the game on TV (delivery/carryout).

To deliver *Quick Service That Sells!* it's important to discover what guests need and want. Asking questions provides this information. Think about salespeople. They ask questions to find out what clients are looking for, then make suggestions to enhance the purchase. A good salesperson would never call on a client without doing research first.

It's a little more difficult in restaurants. In most cases, you don't know who or how many are coming, or what the specific needs are. The crew must be able to determine those needs on the spot to provide the best experience possible. You have only a series of three-second sizzle opportunities.

Don't get caught up in making generalizations about guests.
If someone has dined with you before, there's no need to give a detailed overview of how the service sequence works — they already know! On the other hand, if someone has never dined with you before, don't assume they know what to do after they order. Do you bring the food to them? If not, how will they know it's ready? Do you provide condiments or is it self-serve? A three-second sizzle explanation will start these new guests off on the right foot.

Now, you may know all of this information, but are your guests receiving this customized level of service? If not, it's high time to train your employees to identify and meet guests' individual needs.

The great Yogi Berra said: "When you get to the fork in the road, pick it up." Generally, there are two "forks" during a typical restaurant visit: Have they been there before? And what other specific needs do they have? Simply determining familiarity will enhance the service provided and put your crew on the way to delivering *Quick Service That Sells!*

REGULAR or FIRST-TIMER?

OTHER SPECIAL NEEDS?

If crew members don't recognize a guest, they can simply ask: "Haven't I seen you in here before?"

If the answer is **yes**:

Thank guests for returning. Inform them of specials, features or new items/deals they may not be aware of.

If the answer is **no**:

Welcome guests. Provide menu guidance, suggest items you are famous for and let them know how the service sequence works (if it isn't easily recognized).

After crew members master this step, they can move on to determining other needs. When providing training in this area, don't overwhelm employees. It's impossible to fix everything in a shift or a day.

In football, you get 10 yards in four plays or fewer and you get to keep going. Think how boring the game would be if teams had only four plays to go the length of the field. It wouldn't be very high scoring or exciting.

Same holds true for a restaurant. Set intermediate goals (first downs). Once the crew meets them, hand out rewards and update the goals. Kids try to complete mazes by starting at the beginning. It leads to dead ends, retracing steps and mistakes. After a few times, however, they start at the end and work backward. When looking to move to a higher level of service, take a similar approach. Don't start where service is today and work toward the goal with minor incremental changes. Be bold! Start at the perfect experience and work back to today.

So what do your different types of guests need?

Regulars

They're your bread and butter. You know who they are. Do your cashiers, drive-thru attendants, phone reps and food production employees who interact with guests? There are two types of regulars: high-frequency (multiple visits per week) and average (multiple visits per month). The key to driving sales is getting the average guests to become high-frequency. But how?

Regulars want recognition. Think about the airlines. They treat their most frequent fliers to the most perks — do you? Regulars know how it's supposed to be. They're forgiving but demand consistency. Keep them loyal and don't ever take them for granted.

How Can You Sizzle?

Recognize your regulars. Welcome them and thank them for returning. Some restaurants have walls of fame with celebrity photos, but are they really the most valuable guests? Old Spaghetti Factory has a plaque in one of its restaurants honoring a guest who has dined there more than 4,000 times ... and counting! Regulars typically have a favorite table, chair or barstool — honor them! Eric Clapton started the memorabilia rage at Hard Rock Café in London by asking to place his guitar over his favorite seat. A free meal, appetizer or dessert on occasion will ensure they keep returning.

Alter suggestions. Since regulars may not look at the menu, they may not be aware of new items or promotions. Alter suggestions: "Since you normally order the chicken sandwich, I thought I'd tell you about a new chicken club you may want to try." Or: "The usual or would you like to try the _____?" Or: "Did you know we also have _____?"

Provide special treatment. Put regulars' pictures on the wall or keep pictures near the register so new employees will know who to pamper. Some companies know their frequent guests by the car they drive: "There's red truck Ken!"

Also try these ideas:

- Introduce new employees to the regulars.
- Invite regulars in for a sneak preview of a new menu item (when you're training the team how to prepare and sell the new item).
- Provide progressive discount cards — the more regulars dine, the more they save.
- Start a VIP program so cardholders receive other special benefits and treatment or an "around-the-menu" card encouraging them to try other items each time they come in.

First Time Guests

They're a blank slate. A tourist. Someone visiting on business. A newcomer to the area. Maybe they're responding to your advertising or heeding a referral from a friend or just dropping by. Win them all over by delivering something better than ordinary.

How Can You Sizzle?

Recommend items you're famous for. "Since you've never been here before, you must try the _____." Or: "You just have to try our _____." Or: "You can't say you've been to _____ without trying the _____." Provide a small free sample of your signature item. Watch the register ring! First-time guests should get to experience things they cannot get anywhere else — your outstanding service and great food.

Reassure selections. While it should be done for all guests, it's critical to let newcomers know they've made the right choice:

> Guest: "I'll try the burrito meal deal."
>
> Cashier: "Excellent choice. It's one of our most popular items."

Provide direction. Let them know how the service system works and don't treat them like a number!

Talk to first-time guests. Introduce yourself and find out a little about them. Thank them for the opportunity to serve them and provide a bounce-back coupon for a future visit. A welcome from the manager is an added plus. Find out what you can do to get them to come back more often.

The goal overall is to drive frequency, to create cheerleaders. To do so, match the service to guests' needs, modifying the steps of service if necessary. Regulars need a different set of suggestions than first-timers. Deliver "serve-us" service and your guests will come back again and again.

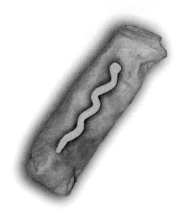

chapter four

Which Path Am I On?

Welcome back my friends to
the show that never ends.

We're so glad you could
attend, come inside, come
inside...

Come inside the show's
about to start

Guaranteed to blow your
head apart...

*Rest assured you'll get your
money's worth*

— *Karn Evil No. 9*
Emerson, Lake and Palmer

Guests are lost by not properly executing the basics — food, service,
cleanliness and atmosphere. If you don't provide these bare-minimum
requirements, you're out of business. And, for the most part, restaurants do a satisfactory job. The basics, however, don't build loyalty.
They're not unique. They don't sizzle.

It's time for the next step on the journey. Once guest frequency has been determined, there are additional needs that may need to be taken into consideration. The following groups fall into the categories discussed in the previous chapter (regulars, first-time guests, etc.) but they have additional needs:

- Families
- Value Diners
- Large Orders
- Seniors
- Special-Needs Guests
- Guests with Dietary Concerns

Families

There has been explosive growth in families dining out or ordering carryout because of two incomes and all the activities kids are involved in. Kids, in fact, continue to drive more and more decisions on where to eat. What restaurants are on the top of their list?

How Can You Sizzle?

Pay attention. Extra napkins or condiments, special requests for "no onions" or "meat and cheese only," help with the kids, providing something to keep the kids busy. Be unique! Make them feel extra special.

Provide fun. What can occupy the kids? The more fun the experience is, the more often the family will return.

Train "kid focus." Many cashiers and other employees don't have children. Their frame of reference may be their pesky little sibling. Teach your crew how to talk to young guests, which includes keeping eye contact at kids' level.

Hit the "tweeners." As kids get to be seven or so, they outgrow kid's meals, but in many cases, Mom and Dad don't want to spring for the adult portion yet. Provide selections for the older child — larger portions of kid's meals (or smaller portions of adult food).

Now That's Quick Service That Sells!

Value Diners

Typically in quick-service restaurants there are a fair share of guests looking for value, using coupons whenever possible or trying to get a deal. They may not appreciate a sales-focused approach, but their money counts the same. A dollar in the register is a dollar not in the competitors'.

How Can You Sizzle?

Make it easy. Simplify the menu. Don't limit value meal purchases to only certain food items. Have the sandwich/burger/taco price on the menu, then allow guests to have the ability make it the appropriate value meal. For example:

○ Add medium fries and a medium drink for $2 extra.

○ Add large fries and a large drink for $3 extra.

○ Add a side salad and a medium drink for $2 extra.

Look at your menu — take the value meal price and subtract out the price of the sandwich. Is it the same price for those fries and drink? Not in most cases, but it should be. Add in the salad option for guests who don't want fries. Make it easier for guests and more profitable for you!

Alter suggestions. Put the information into value-friendly terms. For example:

○ "The best value we have on the menu is the 20-piece chicken tenders."

○ "We have two sizes of value meals. You can order the larger one or save 49 cents and get the regular size. Which would you prefer?"

○ "You can get two pizzas for $15.99 or order one and save $5."

These simple suggestions can turn guests who used to be thought of as high-maintenance into ones singing praises of the restaurant. Make them feel good about getting deals.

> *Now That's* Quick Service That Sells!

Large Orders

Large orders may not be the norm in your operation, but when they do occur, there's probably a specific reason for them: Is it an office meeting? Birthday party sleepover? Team celebration? Find out and sizzle.

How Can You Sizzle?

Throw in random acts of kindness. Find out what the occasion is and drop a "Hope you have a great meeting!" or "Happy Birthday!" or "Hope your team wins!" message in with the order.

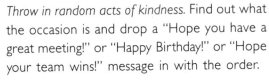

Guests who are celebrating have higher expectations than those just eating a meal. Don't let your crew members give off the impression they're making "just another order." Imagine parents in the delivery room ready to have a baby and the doctor acts like it's no big deal. How would they feel? Guests should hear: "Thanks for allowing us to help with your special occasion."

> *Now That's* Quick Service That Sells!

Seniors

Depending on the clientele, there may be quite a few seniors who dine at your restaurant. Their tendency as a group is to be loyal, but how can you satisfy their needs?

While at Chick-Fil-A one Saturday, I witnessed *Quick Service That Sells!* at its finest. An elderly couple had a coupon for a free grilled chicken salad with the purchase of a large soft drink. The total was $1.69. How many places would think "cheap guests" and blow them off? After all, they really aren't helping build business that day. Heck, the store is probably losing money on the transaction.

Instead, sizzle happened: The lady asked for an extra plate to split the salad, and an extra cup to split the soft drink. Any typical restaurant would have given a hundred reasons why they weren't allowed to do that. After all, $1.69 for two people to eat? The cashier gladly gave them the plate and cup and the guests sat down to enjoy their meal. They felt like a million dollars and I've proceeded to tell this story to plenty of others.

Now That's Quick Service That Sells!

How Can You Sizzle?

Personalize service. Some seniors may want to chat, others may want to have a little privacy. If silent service is called for, deliver it. If guests are talkative, return the favor. Chances are they'll be in every day.

Offer smaller portions. While there may not be an official senior's menu, provide off-the-menu meals with smaller portions, or allow seniors to split a meal (or order a kid's meal). Don't publicize splitting a meal, but if guests inquire it's a great opportunity to create loyalty by making them feel special. Does it cost a little? Sure, but three visits per week at $8 per couple is worth more than $10 once a month. My grandmother was always loyal to places where she thought she was pulling one over on them. It was a small price for the restaurant to pay for a lifetime of loyalty and far cheaper than attracting new guests.

Avoid slang. Slang terms may not be understood or appreciated by seniors or other guests, for that matter. Stress the importance of respectful language. "Yes, ma'am or sir," "My pleasure" and "We'd be happy to" will make all the difference in the world. Talk to me, thank me, appreciate me. Phrases to avoid: cool, awesome, dude, like (as in, "It's like the best we have, dude"), fixin' to and still workin' on that. Provide the respect and treatment seniors desire.

Special-Needs Guests

Guests who are pregnant, have babies or small children in tow, need assistance getting around or are dining alone present a valuable opportunity. Treat them normally, even if you have to make accommodations. Make them feel like every other guest — outstanding!

How Can You Sizzle?

Use common sense. If guests are in a wheel chair or need assistance walking, bring them their food, get their drinks (even if it's self-service), ask if they need extra condiments.

Set for success. Braille menus and room for wheel chairs or carts are simple measures to take ahead of time for special-needs guests. See if they want to sit close to the restroom or an exit, or away from stairs if they need assistance walking.

Now That's Quick Service That Sells!

Guests with Dietary Concerns

Growing interest in low-carb and other fad diets, awareness of food allergies and food quality, and preoccupations with weight watching have created a new segment of guests demanding that you customize food to suit their needs. No longer are vegetarian options enough.

How Can You Sizzle?

Provide information. Guests want to know: Are there peanuts in this item? MSG? Animal enzymes? Is it kosher? How many grams of fat? Is there any gluten in it? Any desserts without sugar? Can I get a low-carb option? Ensure the crew is educated in these areas or at least knows where to go to find out the information. Creating an FAQ sheet or dietary-concern section on the POS terminal can be helpful. At your next meeting, conduct training on how to create low-carb options, or educate the crew on food allergies and prevalent dietary fads. Some restaurants even arm employees with PDAs containing all dietary and food allergy information so they can immediately answer guests' questions.

Now That's Quick Service That Sells!

Be flexible. Guests want to be able to make special requests. If they're turned down, off they go to a more willing competitor. Special-order charges frustrate guests. After all, if they order a burger with no bun, they're saving the restaurant money. Win some, lose some. Price it into the menu to minimize or eliminate up-charges.

Respect everyone. While employees may not agree with an expressed viewpoint at the table, they should respect it. Vegetarians should provide the experience meat eaters want — and vice versa.

"The veggie burger is a popular alternative" works far better than "I don't know, I prefer real meat patties."

Listen. Pay attention to special orders. Ask employees what they're hearing from guests with dietary concerns. Use the feedback to customize the menu or the training to address these needs. Encourage cashiers to ask if there are any special dietary concerns at the outset of the meal.

Variety is the spice of life. By providing customized service, your cashiers, phone reps and drive-thru attendants won't be bored and all your different guests will have a great time. Celebrate the differences and reap the rewards.

chapter five

The Drive-Thru (or drive-in) Experience

"Never go through the drive-thru! **They *$&! you in the drive-thru.**"

Joe Pesci in Lethal Weapon 2

For those restaurant chains that offer drive-thru service, chances are it is responsible for more than 60 percent of the business. Face it, today's consumer wants convenience and staying in the car is often preferred. But does it sizzle? Guests hate to be processed but give restaurants a little slack in this area. After all, they are being catered to by not having to get out of their car.

How important is the drive-thru to your business? Some industry leaders have stated saving six seconds per car equals a 1 percent sales increase! But in the quest to enhance times, don't forget about the other critical areas — quality, accuracy and a dose of hospitality.

To understand how speed matters:

30 cars per half-hour

 $5 ticket average

= $150 per half-hour

---

40 cars per half-hour

X $5 ticket average

= $200 per half-hour

If there are two peak hours at lunch and another two at dinner, a $50 increase per half-hour over the four hours equals $400 in additional sales per day!

The sizzle points are numerous, but often ignored if you fail to venture outside the four walls. Check the following opportunities to sizzle:

- Approach and Loop
- Menu Board
- Ordering Process
- Food Delivery and Payment Process

All these areas impact the guests' perception of your restaurant. **Amost two-thirds of guests experience these sizzle points,** but how much of your time are you spending on them? Before examining the sizzle points, a few basics for drive-thru success:

- Aces in their places! If the drive-thru represents 60 percent of the business, have the top players working the key positions.
- Keep condiments and all supplies well-stocked.
- Utilize all preparation areas during peak times.
- Track drive-thru times and monitor business throughout the shift — without getting stuck working the position (don't forget about the dine-in business!).

In addition, analyze what processes may slow drive-thru times. **Ensure your system focuses on quality and accuracy first, then speed.** Many changes can address speed of service, but if these systems sacrifice quality and accuracy, it will harm long-term business.

Implement changes to remove bottlenecks. First, explore the use of technology: drive-thru timers, order confirmation boards, additional headsets, POS systems that suggest items to round the total up to the next dollar, dedicated credit card terminals and phone lines to speed credit transactions, or even self-swipe technology similar to pay-at-the-pump in gas stations.

Let's examine each sizzle point a little more closely:

Typical Approach and Loop

- Trash strewn in landscaping and in driveway/parking lot.
- Dirty dumpster visible.
- Marks on walls, chipped paint.
- Signage inconsistent or messy.
- Slow moving line.

Quick Service That Sells! Approach and Loop

- Landscape well manicured.
- Parking lot spotless and well maintained.
- Dumpster area clean, hosed down and/or enclosed.
- Building immaculate.
- Signage professional-looking and clean.
- Line is long because everyone knows it moves quickly.

Now That's Quick Service That Sells!

First impressions create lasting impressions — don't be fooled! Go through your drive-thru loop and see what guests see, especially at the sight lines. How clean do they perceive your restaurant to be on the inside if they see trash, debris and deterioration on the outside?

Guests notice and often just drive by, never giving you another chance. Once they pull the car into the line, they expect speed. The menu board and ordering process help determine how quickly they'll get through the line.

Typical Menu Board and Ordering Process

- Menu cluttered, hard to read or understand.
- Speaker clarity unclear, volume not correct.
- Drive-thru attendant not helpful with indecisive guests — line backs up.
- No guidance if guest orders an item which takes extra time to prepare.
- Order not repeated back (was it right?).
- Total is not given.
- Kitchen begins order once it shows up on the monitor or printer.

Quick Service That Sells! Menu Board and Ordering Process

- Menu clean and easy to read. For example, photo/graphic heavy versus words; "Make any sandwich a medium value meal for only $2 extra or a large value meal for $3 extra" — ease of ordering equals faster drive-thru times.
- Order-taker working the line during peak times — either providing menus (highlighting key deals) to cars prior to the menu board or taking the order of every other car and calling it back to the drive-thru attendant. Orders are taken twice as fast, more friendly and with more effective suggestions.
- Drive-thru attendant offers suggestions (quickly!) to indecisive guests and informs guests of items with long preparation times. (In those cases, guests may decide to order something else, or at least be prepared for the additional wait time.)
- Order is repeated back (or confirmation board is used).
- Total is provided along with a request for condiments: "Your total is $4.79. Would you like any ketchup (or salsa, etc.) with your order?"
- Kitchen line person is wearing a headset so he or she can begin making the order right away.

Now That's Quick Service That Sells!

Now it's time to get face to face with guests.

Typical Food Delivery and Payment Process

- Monotone cashier says the total — guest pays.
- Drive-thru attendant casually gets change.
- Drive-thru attendant passes bag out the window and shuts it.
- If the order is not ready, guest is told to park in one of the designated spaces for drive-thru.
- Guest delays pulling away from window — undoubtedly something is incorrect or missing (speed is slowed down).

Quick Service That Sells! Food Delivery and Payment Process

- Welcoming drive-thru attendant who greets guests: "Having a great day? Your food will be ready in just a second!" (Three seconds of hospitality while the order is prepared certainly makes the time pass by faster.)
- Makes eye contact and smiles.
- Change is ready to be provided. For example, if the total is $4.79, 21 cents is ready to be handed out.
- Orders are confirmed as they're handed out. Since the order-taker already asked if condiments were needed, they're in the bag.
- If the order is not ready, it is brought to the guest with a little perk such as a larger drink or fries.
- Drive-thru attendant thanks guests and invites them back soon: "Thanks again — see you tomorrow!" or "We appreciate the business — don't forget to try the _____ next time!"
- Guests know it is right and will return.

*Now **That's** Quick Service That Sells!*

Don't forget to listen to your crew members. Are they sizzling guests? Delivering hospitality and suggestive selling? If not, review the respective chapters of this book and role play with the team so you can move your sales and service levels higher.

How is your system working today? What is your drive-thru time? Accuracy in filling orders? Many of the leading companies consistently move guests from speaker box to departure in two to three minutes or less. Many companies track "at the window" time (where guests pick up the food) and are consistently hitting 20 to 30 seconds.

Some restaurants have even posted a guarantee: "If your order isn't delivered within 30 seconds of pulling up to the window, it's free!" Having guests watch a timer heightens the sense of urgency. Don't ever forget quality and accuracy, however!

Leading chains exceed 90 percent in filling orders properly. The most missed items? **Condiments, napkins, incorrect drinks and special requests not executed properly.** While 90 percent is an "A" in school, that's still one out of 10 incorrect orders! The top performing QSR company averages only one mistake per 3,300 orders.

Now That's Quick Service That Sells!

chapter six

Delivery and Carryout Sizzle

"Answer the phone,
it's a guest calling!"

Today's delivery and carryout business (pizza, Chinese food, wings, etc.) creates a separate set of sizzle points. Additionally, the playing field has become very crowded with not only the traditional places, but also full-service restaurants offering carryout. How can your operation stand apart and dominate?

First of all, leverage your strengths. You may not have the array of menu options like casual-dining restaurants offering takeout, but you can out-execute them! Their strength is the dine-in experience, not taking orders over the phone. It's at this sizzle point where you can shine, as well as when guests pick up or receive their orders.

You can also take advantage of guests' carryout or delivery expectations, which typically are low. Get the order right, maintain the proper temperature and deliver it on time — do just those things and guests are pretty satisfied. Satisfied, yes. Sizzle, no.

The key sizzle points in a take-out/delivery operation are:

- The Phone (a.k.a. the sales engine)
- Order Pick-up/Carryout
- Delivery
- Follow-up

The lifeline to your guests is the phone and POS system. Many operations have POS systems which include caller ID integrated with the ordering system so the operator can view order history, address, etc. Talk about an advantage (if utilized properly)! Most casual-dining restaurants don't have this tracking mechanism. People simply call up and place an order. Use this to your advantage. Otherwise, you're just like everyone else!

Execute the following steps better than any other competitor:

1) Greet guests with something unique.
2) Receive the order.
3) Use "Situational Selling" to enhance the meal selections (more on this in the next chapter).
4) Repeat the order to ensure accuracy.
5) Be quick, but not too quick — another guest wants to experience the awesome service you provide. Balance speed with sales suggestions (one to two max).

Telephone

Deliver three-second sizzle over the phone and you have a guest for life who enjoys spending money with you.

Typical Phone Interactions

- Phone answered robotically or so quickly that callers don't know to whom they're talking.
- Immediately put on "ignore" (the next level of hold).
- Treated as an interruption of business.
- Treated the same (average, at best) no matter how many times a particular guest has ordered.
- "Delivery or carryout?" or "Hold, please" are the first words spoken.
- Callers are processed for the sake of speed.
- No suggestive selling (unless you count "Anything else?").
- Insincerely states total (if caller is lucky) as well as the estimated delivery or pickup time.
- Lacking knowledge about directions, hours of operation or answers to FAQs.

Quick Service That Sells! Phone Interactions

- Friendly voice welcomes the guest with a personalized greeting and identifies potential needs: "Thanks for calling (location)! Today we are featuring _____ as well as a number of other specials. Would you like to hear about them?"

- Use guests' names. If you don't have caller ID, you can collect their phone number or name so you can access it in the POS system or record it for delivery.

- Customize the call. Identify the high-frequency users or first-time callers. Again, if the POS system doesn't provide the information for you, ask! Thank the frequent user for being loyal and throw in random acts of kindness (a free sample of the new dessert or appetizer you're offering). For first-time callers, suggest your most popular items and provide guidance on the menu such as deals or special offers.

○ Ask how many people the caller is ordering for so the specials can be customized. Just as a couple placing an order doesn't want to hear about the three-large-pizza or 100-wing special, bigger groups need to hear about the larger size offerings so sales aren't lost by suggesting smaller-sized specials. Sell to the situation.

○ Once callers have finished their order, suggest additional items to complete and enhance the meal. Don't keep the caller on the phone too long. Didn't order an appetizer or dessert? Offer a choice of two and ask which they would prefer.

○ Sales tips sound guest-friendly. For example, if a caller orders a medium one-topping pizza, a sizzle reply would be: "We're featuring two pizzas for $13.99 or you can save $4 and order one for $9.99" or "We're offering a special deal: one pizza, an appetizer of your choice and a two-liter bottle of soda for $14.99 or the pizza by itself is $9.99 — which would you like to do?"

○ Phone rep listens for cues. If it's a large order, ask what the occasion is. Then add a personalized card that highlights the event: "Happy Birthday! Enjoy the pizza."

○ The order is repeated back, the total is confirmed, and callers are informed, by name, that a friendly delivery person will be at their door soon (or within a quoted time).

○ Phone rep can answer questions about directions from major intersections, hours of operation, menu, specials, promotions, etc.

Now That's Quick Service That Sells!

Depending on the type of business, carryout or pick-up may make up a large or small percentage of your total sales. Sizzling when guests arrive to pick up food is a prime opportunity to solidify loyalty.

Typical Carryout/Pick-up Interactions

- Guests treated like an interruption.
- No greeting at all or welcomed with that oh-so-personal: "Phone number?" or "Name?"
- No hospitality or interaction if there's a wait.
- Order is handed over, payment is taken.
- Another ho-hum experience.

Quick Service That Sells! Carryout/Pick-up Interactions

- Guests are welcomed as they enter.
- Employees interact with guests.
- A drink is offered if there's a wait (suggest a 20-oz soda).
- Order is confirmed (open the box if it's a pizza or show guests their order in the bag).
- Bounce-back coupon is offered.
- Payment tendered and guest personally thanked: "Thanks again Mr./Ms. _____ See you again next week!"

Now That's Quick Service That Sells!

If your restaurant delivers, some control of the experience is lost. After all, the delivery driver is not interacting with the guest inside the restaurant. Teaching and role-playing delivery sizzle is critical. Otherwise, it may end up something like this:

Typical Delivery
- Indifferent employee arrives: "Here's your order."
- No mention of the coupons on the box or in the bag.
- Order is not confirmed.
- Guests are not thanked.

Quick Service That Sells! Delivery
- Enthusiastic driver greets guest.
- Uses guest's name.
- Describes order using descriptive words.
- Points out coupons on box or in bag and encourages guest to use them soon!
- Thanks guest!

Now That's Quick Service That Sells!

Finally, the follow-up. Yes, follow-up, as in call guests the following day to see how their meal and service were. After all, how do you really know? Just because they don't call to complain doesn't mean the service rocked. Silence is deadly.

Add a new step to the opening checklist:

> Call three to five of yesterday's orders to check on the experience. Expected? No. Sizzle? You bet! Will those guests be calling a competitor the next time? Hardly.

A few other marketing sizzle points:

- If the POS system tracks usage by guest, run a report ranking guests by dollars spent. Take the top 20 or 25 and drop them a personal thank-you note letting them know how important they are to your business. Don't forget to drop in a free meal coupon!

- Along the same lines, print a report listing those guests who haven't ordered from the restaurant in the last 60 or 90 days. Put a "We want you back" postcard in the mail or call them to find out why they no longer do business with you. Not only will you be able to uncover past problems (and repair them), those guests will know they aren't just another number.

- Create a "street of the week" flier or residential door hanger. Pick streets in your neighborhood and include a special offer that must be redeemed within a short time period.

- Have delivery drivers write their name or a code on coupons for their deliveries. Reward the person who gets the most redeemed. Funny the correlation between great service and repeat business!

Now That's Quick Service That Sells!

Situational Selling

S.A.L.E.S. — Sell A Little Extra Something

Many guests are tired of pushy sales crews. Why? When suggestions are not made in the appropriate fashion or at the right time, they seem insincere and mechanical. It's been called "suggestive selling," "informing," "up-selling," "permission selling," "right selling" and so on. It's evolved to "situational selling."

Sell what guests need to buy, not what you want to sell. The goal may be to sell as many super-deluxe loaded burgers, tacos or pizzas as possible, but many guests rarely buy it. So why ask everyone? Focus your energy and sales tactics in areas where you have the greatest chance of success. There is no one-size-fits-all answer.

Before delving into specifics,
take a look at the types of selling:

Upselling

Suggestive Selling

Situational Selling

○ *Upselling* is enhancing an item already ordered (such as upsizing a value meal, adding an additional pizza, suggesting cheese on a burger or adding guacamole to a taco, nachos or a burrito).

○ *Suggestive selling* is describing an item guests have not ordered yet.

○ *Situational selling* is assessing the situation and *informing* guests of items or deals that best enhance that situation (let guests make the choice).

Knowing why guests are paying a visit makes it easier to sell. Lose the monotone "Would you like to up-size your value meal?" and insincere "I have to tell you about our _____ or we get counted off by our mystery shopper" or "Would you like to add another pizza for $4?"

Is there any benefit to the guests in the previous situations? Suggesting enhancements to the meal is a key step in the cycle of service, but the practice needs to be subject to interpretation. While guests may not like to deal with pushy salespeople, there is no doubt they like to spend money and buy things they like or want. Make it easy for guests to say yes.

For example, regulars may not look at the menu (or don't have one if they are calling in). They know what they want — right? Can you skip the suggestion step? Sure, if you want to lose revenue!

Consider: A man calls to order pizza for his family. He orders the typical large pepperoni. Next time he's driving by the restaurant he notices the two-fer' deal as well as the new chicken tenders being offered. "I wish I knew about those offers."

Moral of the story: Alter suggestions to the situation: "Were you aware we now have a two-pizza special as well as chicken tenders? Which would you prefer?" or "Many guests are now adding chicken tenders to their pizza order — they are out of this world."

Another reason cashiers or phone reps don't sell is they lack confidence. Why? They don't have enough knowledge. If, for instance, they haven't been trained well on the menu (or the training was so long ago it's been forgotten), they're not likely to suggest these items. They're afraid they won't know an answer to guests' questions.

So what can be done to increase knowledge? Train them! The employees don't need to be experts on every ingredient and flavor profile, but they do need to be able to suggest items confidently and answer questions that guests may have. Simple ideas such as a daily sampling, item-of-the-day discussions before the shift or recipe-card reviews will help the crew become more valuable to the guests and you!

> Here are other ideas to help situational selling become a reality:

Ask questions. If guests are indecisive, ask what they typically order or what type of food they like so you can customize suggestions and ensure they have an outstanding meal.

Suggest unique items. Everyone offers standard fare, and it should be on the menu, but to get guests coming back again and again, it's a good idea to let them know about items they can't get anywhere else. Or maybe it's the method of preparation that sets a familiar dish apart. In other words, promote what makes your food distinctive.

Eliminate questions such as "Would you like..." and *"Do you want.."* They virtually encourage a "no" response. For example, "Would you like an appetizer?" If guests are indecisive, "no" is the easy way out. Or perhaps they'll decline because there are too many unanswered questions: "How much is it?" and "What do you have?" and "Which one is the best?"

When you don't make it easy for guests to see the benefits, expect "no." What's more, the proper answer to "What's good here?" is not "Everything." Guests want direction. What are they in the mood for? What type of food are they craving? Information is power. Power to deliver *Quick Service That Sells!*

Watch the negatives. Since most cashiers sell like they've been sold to, they tend to repeat what they hear when they eat out. Unfortunately, many of those phrases are negative and may have crept into their vocabulary. When was the last time you actually listened to one of your cashiers or phone reps make suggestions?

Post a sign in the break area or on the POS terminal with a big red X through these phrases:

"You don't want to upsize that (or add another pizza) do you?"

"Anything else?"

"Decided yet?"

"Is that all?"

Offer a choice of two. Use "Which would you prefer?" instead of "Would you like...?" It's not selling as much as it is informing guests of their choices and letting them decide. For example:

Value Meals

Guest: "I'll have a burger value meal."

Cashier: "The large value meal is $4.99 or you can save 49 cents and get the regular size meal. Which sounds good to you?"

Pizza Deals

Guest: "I'll have a large pepperoni pizza."

Phone rep: "You can get two large one-topping pizzas for $13.99 or save $4 and get one for $9.99. Which would you like?"

Desserts

Guest: "That's all."

Cashier: "We have two great desserts, _____ and _____. Which would you like to add for only $1?"

Inform guests about favorites or promotions. Pointing out value can be helpful, too. Sell the benefit to guests. Let them buy what they want, not what you're trying to sell. Effective phrases are:

- "Which breakfast sandwich would you like with your coffee?"
- "My favorite sandwich is the _____."
- "Our most popular deals are _____."
- "If you're really hungry, I'd recommend the _____."
- "Were you aware we also serve _____?"
- "The least expensive way to do that is _____."
- "For a group that size, I'd suggest _____."
- "If it were me, I'd get the _____."
- "If you want low carbs, may I suggest the _____."
- "If you're looking for something low-cal, the best tasting item would be the _____."

Remind crew to say it in guests' terms. For example, "The best value is the large size meal or you can save a few cents and get the regular size," or "The most popular deal is two medium pizzas for $13.99 or you can save a few dollars and get one for $9.99."

Keep score. Retail chains routinely post sales ticket averages, as well as the highest total sales on a quarterly or annual basis. Imagine your cashiers' faces when they see their total sales for the year are more than $100,000 or they have the top ticket average in the store, district or whole chain. Information is power — the power to deliver *Quick Service That Sells!*

Situational selling is based on the confidence to guide guests to yes. Success requires training. There's an old story about a couple of shoe salespeople who get sent to a remote area to sell shoes to the tribes people. The first salesperson calls in to the supervisor and says: "No opportunity here — nobody wears shoes." The second salesperson calls in to the supervisor and says: "An incredible opportunity here — nobody wears shoes!"

Now That's Quick Service That Sells!

chapter eight

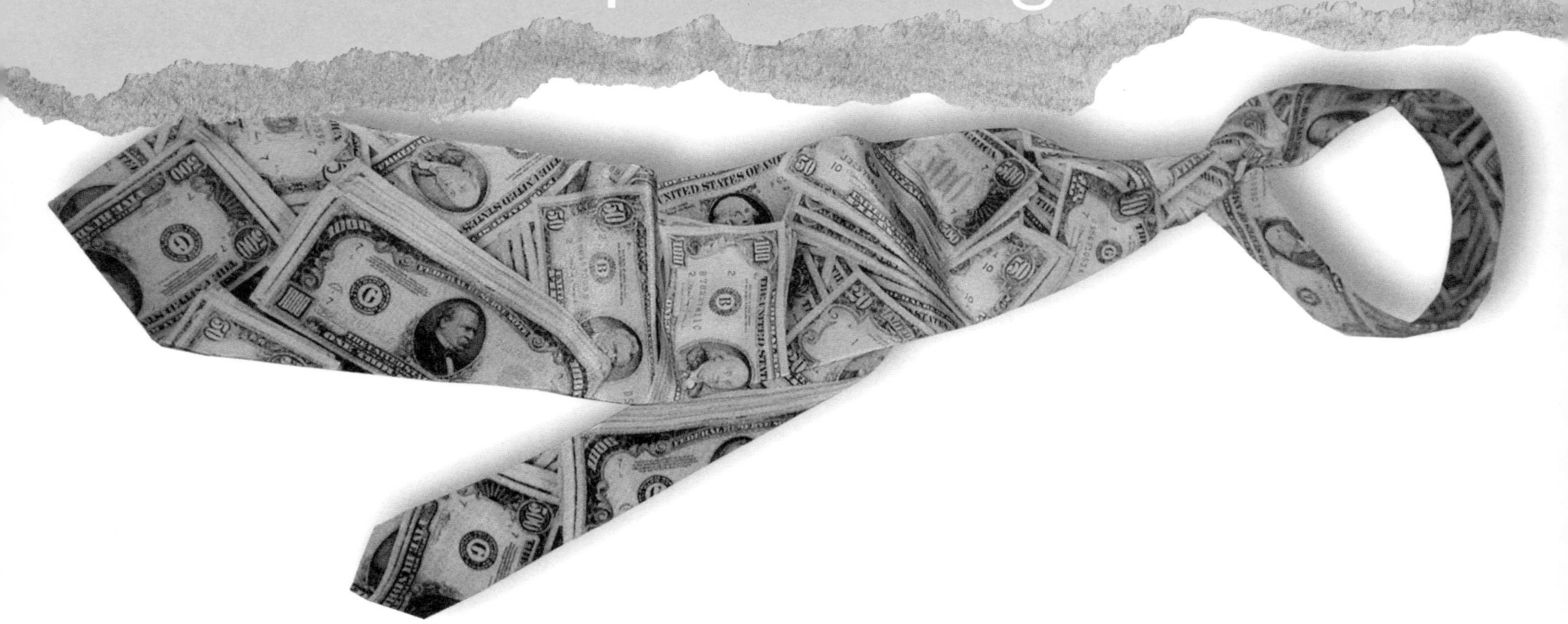

The Manager (That's You!)

It's the singer, not the song
*that makes the music move
along.*

"Join Together with the Band" —
The Who

Face it, most restaurants provide decent food, fair prices, OK service and typically get the order correct. So what truly separates one from another? Take a look in the mirror, baby. It's the manager on duty — *you!* — who makes the biggest difference.

You determine if employees look sharp. You set the tone and expectations of service. So ask yourself: Do you run the shift or does the shift run you? Do you make it happen, watch it happen or wonder what happened?

Chain restaurants have numerous locations with the same building design and menu, similar people and advertising. Yet some run better than others. Why? The manager on duty (M.O.D.).

Managers, owners, franchisees — all make shifts happen! To drive change effectively, it's wise to exaggerate the actions needed. Think about how hard it is to start pedaling a bike. Moving a gear initially takes extra effort but becomes easier as it gathers momentum. The same holds true when moving your crew in a new direction.

Create the buzz and the energy. Get the crew primed for the show and keep it revved up the entire time.

Leading the charge and setting the example are the first steps. If the team isn't improving every day, the competition is catching up or passing by. There are numerous sizzle points managers can execute with guests. In many quick-service style restaurants, if managers interact with guests at all, it's from a position (cashier, drive-thru, phone rep, picking up an order).

Typical Manager Interactions
  o Mechanical, robotic and scripted.
  o Filling an hourly position.
  o Questions asked are general: "How is everything?"

If guests respond "All right" or "OK," are those answers acceptable? Many of your competitors think so. Parts of the visit may be great, others average and some not so good. When they're all rolled up, they're merely "OK." Managers learn nothing but feel good because they hear no complaints about what's really happening.

Quick Service That Sells! **Manager Interactions**
  o Questions asked are specific.
  o "Are your burgers/tacos/wings delicious?"
  o "I understand it is your first time here. What brought you in?"
  o "How did you find out about us?"
  o "What could we do to get you in more frequently?"
  o Eye contact made with guests, perhaps down at their level.
  o Children get complimented (how they color, how well they ate, how they did in their game today if they are wearing a uniform).
  o Responses and cues listened for: OK is not OK.

Now That's Quick Service That Sells!

An effective manager truly values guests' business, personally demonstrating that they're not just a number or a step on a checklist. When running the pulse check in your own operation, rub elbows with guests at multiple points and look for opportunities to wow them.

Working the Line
- "Glad to see you."
- "Just a few more minutes. Don't forget to order the
  _____."

Thanking Departing Guests
- "Great to see you again!"
- "We appreciate you coming in tonight! Tell all your friends."
- "See you tomorrow!"

The Beverage/Condiment Bar
- "Do we have your favorite selections?"
- "Is there anything else I can get you?"

Meals Not Eaten
- "Was _____ not prepared to your liking?"
- "May I get you something else?"
- Fix the problem or take it off the bill.

At the Table
- Have a purpose and reason to be there. Find out information to help drive business.
- Refill drinks.
- Remove trash or unneeded items. For example, "Are you still enjoying the _____ or may I remove it?"
- Find out how service has been.
- Promote specials or marketing initiatives currently going on.
- Provide a bounce-back coupon.

○ Have guests fill out a contact card to be mailed or e-mailed specials and coupons.

○ What else can we do to build frequency?

○ Any part of the visit just OK or ordinary?

Table visits tend to be an interruption of guests' visits. Use the time instead to build sales and relationships. Along the way, you'll minimize the big complaints. And, if an experience does fall short and you've already visited the guests, they won't be as angry. Don't think of these interactions as complaints. They are opportunities to learn, improve, recover and turn the guest into a marketing and salesperson for your operation.

Guests, in fact, often want to make management "aware of something" versus "complaining." You will hear more feedback if the guests know you care. Rather than walk out, never to return, they throw out the opportunity to resolve the situation. A little thing at first could become a big thing if left unaddressed.

Speaking of complaints, everything doesn't always come up roses. There'll be times when guests simply aren't satisfied. Remember, the competition is shooting for "satisfied" and is happy with "OK." In your world, falling a little short of "outstanding" is far better than reaching "OK." When guests let you know of an issue, do you view it as an opportunity to sizzle or cringe at the sound of another complaint?

Typical Responses to Odd Requests or Complaints

- "No."
- "Can't do that."
- "Only if you pay more."
- "It's our policy."
- "You ordered it that way."
- "You didn't ask it if came with onions."

Quick Service That Sells! Responses

- "Yes, for a small additional charge we would be happy to do that."
- "Another way to do that would be..."
- "The best way to ensure you are seated quickly is..."
- "What I can do for you is..."

Now That's Quick Service That Sells!

Employees' responses must be positive. Yet they typically don't know how to do it when they begin working. Why? When they eat (or order) out, they're treated negatively. Managers must model and train for the desired behaviors. If they don't practice this philosophy, the employees certainly won't. Look in the mirror — do you believe it? Are you passionate about it?

Empower your employees to respond properly to any kind of request. To be successful, they'll need the training and the autonomy to make good decisions. You'll need to support them, even if they make mistakes from time to time. In those cases, it's wise to discuss the matter privately, never in front of guests. A good way to start: "What could we have done differently to prevent the situation from occurring?"

Employees who can solve problems and know they have the backing of management will provide great service. Fries are cold? Drink is wrong? Sandwich or pizza made incorrectly? Employees can take care of these situations. If the manager has to get involved, use this acronym:

L.E.A.S.T.

Listen, Empathize, Apologize, Solve, Thank

Listen. Many guests simply want to vent their frustrations and know that someone has heard them.

Empathize. Not sympathize ("I feel bad for you"). Empathize ("If that happened to me, I'd also be upset"). Repeat back the issues to guests to make sure they're understood.

Apologize. Many times "I'm sorry" will make the problem all better. When the restaurant falls short of expectations, guests deserve an apology.

Solve. Fix the problem. Explain the fix to the guest. It will help them see you truly care and that you are learning and changing due to their input. Many managers try to buy guests off. An insincere comp, however, won't cut it if guests don't feel like the problem is solved. Example: "I'm sorry we were out of toilet paper, here's a coupon for a free dessert." The freebie won't be used if guests don't return.

Thank. Thank guests for bringing the situation to light. It's an opportunity to build loyalty. Thousands of people leave restaurants each day unhappy and never return. Silence isn't golden!

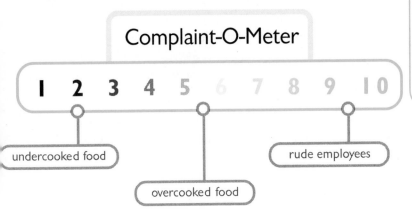

Complaint-O-Meter

1 2 3 4 5 6 7 8 9 10

undercooked food

overcooked food

rude employees

Hospitality expert Jim Newberry suggests using the "complaint-o-meter." Judge complaints on a scale of one to 10 — always from guests' point of view. A hair in food may be a two to you, but a 10 to the guest. If you act like it's no big deal, the meter could run up to 20. Once you ascertain the level of the complaint, the proper resolution can be provided.

Items lower on the meter (in the eyes of the guest) can usually be resolved with immediate action, listening, apologizing and manager involvement. Buying their meal doesn't solve the problem. An undercooked burger or pizza, on the other hand, can be quickly fixed.

Items in the middle of the meter require compensation. An overcooked pizza or chicken fingers cannot be quickly fixed and the guest will not be eating while the rest of his or her party is. Deducting the meal off the bill, a free meal for a future visit or a free dessert are good options.

Complaints on the high end of the meter — rude employees and foreign objects in food, for example — may require a full comp ... plus! Don't stop until guests say: "No you don't have to do that. Really, that's enough."

Be careful not to create a standard resolution policy such as: Food took too long equals free dessert. Food not cooked properly equals comp. And so on. It should be clear by now that **every guest and every situation is different.**

Guests don't want you to disrespect their time. Even providing a refund for a 10 on the complaint-o-meter may not be enough for a ruined meal. Be unique and ensure the situation is resolved to their satisfaction.

Additionally, leave the P&L out of the equation. Comping a dinner may seem like it cost the $6 menu price, but, in actuality, it was $2 worth of food. Providing a free meal on a future visit doesn't cost the full retail value — only the actual cost of items provided.

There'll always be a small percentage of guests out to scam you. The vast majority, though, want to spend money — let them! Guests using an expired coupon — it's OK. No attitude from employees, just a simple "My pleasure." The guests will be back and more loyal than ever!

*Now **That's** Quick Service That Sells!*

The last — and quite large — piece of the managerial puzzle is profitability. Volumes have been written on the subject to help save a nickel here and there. The focus has been bringing in the dollars. No sense regurgitating a bunch of well-worn rhetoric on dumpster dives and trash digs for silverware.

Let's aim the thought process on the largest controllable expense — labor. Yes, cutting labor has an immediate short-term impact on the bottom line, and there are plenty of right times and reasons for managers to make the call. Trying to deliver *Quick Service That Sells!* may seem costly at first blush and initial reactions from district managers and area supervisors may be: "Not this month." Look at it from a different angle before rushing to a decision.

There are two ways to increase profitability: raise sales or lower expenses. In many cases, labor expense needs to be adjusted down. But what if you want to add hours to the schedule to enhance service levels? First, see where labor hours are not needed and can be re-allocated to more productive times. If there's still a need for more hours, look at two things:

Ticket averages. If all the best cashiers, drive-thru attendants or phone reps were working on the same shift (ideally the busiest ones), how much higher would sales be than what the current team is producing? If the restaurant serves 250 guests during a dinner shift and has a ticket average only 50 cents higher, $125 in additional sales is generated. The additional sales keep labor in line (or even lower it) while keeping the restaurant fully staffed to provide wow experiences for guests who, in turn, will return more frequently.

Return on investment. If crew needs to be added to ensure *Quick Service That Sells!* happens, let everyone know how much sales must be increased to provide the ROI necessary to compensate for the additional labor.

Example:

> Let's say you want to place an order-taker in line or in the drive-thru (or add another phone rep to take phone orders). Sales and service levels are adequate, at best. You want to add personnel to ensure the line moves more quickly or answer more calls so they don't go to the competitor. To cover the peak hours, two additional employees are necessary. Hourly labor typically runs at 18 percent. What additional sales must be generated to justify the labor?

2 employees **X** $7 per hour each **X** 2 hours

= $28 of additional labor

Sales necessary to maintain labor % ($28/18%) **= $156**

How do the two additional employees make up the $156? Ensuring more people get through the line (or calls are answered more promptly) will ensure sales are increased. When business heats up, cars or callers go to the competition if the restaurant can't get them handled quickly. Additionally, cashiers or phone reps simply process the line quickly and forget to sell.

So how can it pay out?

Drive-Thru

30 cars per half-hour at $5 ticket average	= $150
40 cars per half-hour at $5 ticket average	= $200
Incremental sales per half-hour	= $50

Two peak hours during the meal period will generate a total sales increase of **$200** — far in excess of the $156 needed to be a good deal.

Delivery/Carryout

45 calls per hour at $14 ticket average	= $630
55 calls per hour at $14 ticket average	= $770
Incremental sale per hour	= $140

Two peak hours during the meal period generates a sales increase of $280 — twice the required amount. Labor decreases significantly!

In addition, having the order-taker working the line or drive-thru (or the additional phone rep answering calls) will certainly allow time to provide better selling opportunities than the current system of rushing guests or callers through the process.

Sales

500 guests per hour at $5 ticket average	= $2,500
500 guests per hour at $5.15 ticket average	= $2,575
Incremental sales per day	= $75
Annual increase in sales	= $27,375

A simple $0.15 ticket average increase generates over $27,000 in annual sales.

There'll likely be a skeptic reading this who says: **"Why would I want to sell items which will raise my food cost?"** Selling desserts or extra cheese on pizzas raises the food cost line. Should those items not be suggested? If you focused on food cost, you wouldn't want these items sold. The additional revenue generated raises top-line sales. Increasing top-line sales lowers the cost percentages per line, as well as raises the profit percentage flowing to the bottom line.

Even if food cost increases 0.1 percent, the additional sales will lower all the other cost lines to ensure the right financial decision is made. Fixed cost items such as salaries, utilities, etc., remain the same whether the item is sold or not, so they decrease on a percentage basis, hence the overall profitability increase.

Don't take the managerial eye off cost controls. Do, however, **open up the focus on how building sales helps increase margins and lower costs.** Otherwise, ineffective business decisions are made. The old saying "Don't trip over dollars to pick up pennies" says it best. Focus on the top line, train the front line, and the dollars will be on the bottom line.

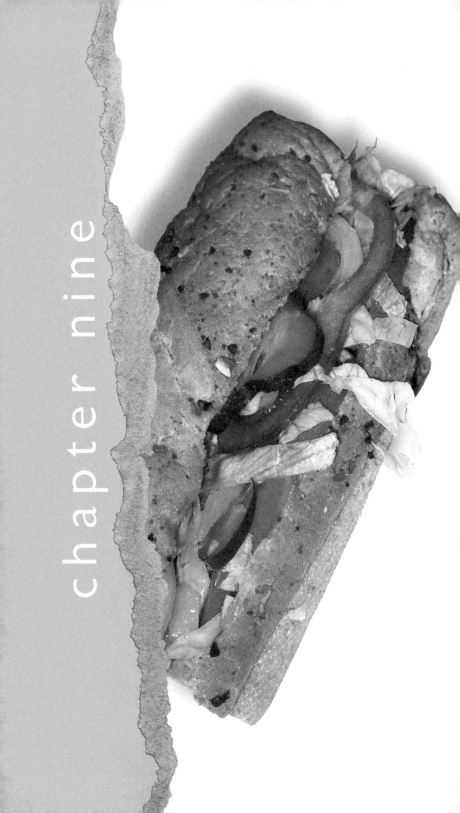

The New Players

Hire me, train me, reward me, retain me.

It's a simple mantra to guide your management of human resources, but what goes wrong? Lack of a top line, too much focus on the bottom line, ignoring good employees, allowing slackers to stay, bad hires, inadequate training, no recognition or appreciation — all of these factors lead to turnover.

To help unravel and solve this mystery, let's start at the beginning. There are four key components to creating a successful restaurant:

- Who you hire.
- How you train them.
- Who trains them.
- The environment they work in.

Old hat? Yesterday's news? Common sense? Retro is back and it's cool. There's a new spin on the old favorites. It used to be slow and boring, but now it's hip, cool, upbeat and geared toward today's employees.

Let's look at each part, starting with hiring. Everyone's heard that hiring is the most important thing you do as a manager. It's more than that. **Hiring the *right person* is the most important thing you do.**

Book after book has been written about hiring, and many companies provide pre-employment testing (Pencom International, 800-247-8514), computer kiosk applications and background checks. While those items certainly help make the right decisions, they're only a piece of the puzzle. So what else can you do?

First, know what to look for. Ask your current employees what adjectives they would use to describe their jobs and put them in your advertisements to attract the right type of applicant. What are the requirements of each position in the restaurant and the skills necessary to do the job? Most restaurants have job descriptions and use them to frame their interview questions. Want to stay where you are? Keep doing it. Ready to move ahead? To take it one step further, assess what skills the best employees have. **Ask employees to write down what they do and the skills necessary to excel.**

Why are they more successful and productive than others? Talk to them to find out why they believe they produce the results they do. Find those same skills and traits in your new hires.

Drill down to specifics. It's not enough to say we need "friendly, outgoing, energetic people." Who doesn't? Most companies' job descriptions for a cashier or line cook look pretty similar. What's the difference between the great and the not-so-great? Usually it's a manager's ability to assess and uncover these skills in an interview.

> Many companies today teach managers how to interview as well as provide the specific questions for managers to ask. It's not the questions, however, that matter the most. It's the answers.

So what skills do employees who can deliver *Quick Service That Sells!* possess? What is their service DNA? All the common ones you could name quickly: outgoing, friendly, hospitable, like to serve others, and so on. But what else do they need?

Keep in mind that an applicant's frame of reference for the duties of a cashier, phone rep or drive-thru attendant is the restaurant up the street. If part of the job description of a cashier is to enter the order, anyone can do that. However, if you want them to deliver hospitality, it requires a different skill set.

Interviews should be thought of as auditions. Have applicants demonstrate the skills necessary versus nodding their head "yes" or "no" to your questions. Ask yourself, too, what specific talents are needed for each position — the intangibles, traits or skills possessed by your great employees. A few to consider:

Cashier/Phone Rep

Sales skills. Do applicants have what it takes to sell? Interview strategy: Have them role play selling a specific item. Ask how they would rate past service experiences, as well as how they would improve them. Sample questions: What are your monetary needs per week? How do you feel you can help achieve those needs? How would you suggest a value meal? Sell me your favorite item (from a previous job or what they like when they dine out).

Integrity. Cashiers handle the cash. They need to ring up every item properly, even when nobody is watching. Sample questions: What would you do if you saw another employee not ringing up an item? If you found an item the guest lost, do you consider it stealing to take it?

Greeting. Can cashier applicants make a wow from the outset? Interview strategy: Pretend you're a guest approaching the register and have them greet you. Would you want this person taking care of you? Look for smiles, eye contact and enthusiasm.

Multi-tasking. Great cashiers received an extra dose of this gene. Look for applicants who are involved in numerous activities and jump from one thing to another. Cashiers have to juggle many things at the same time. Sample questions: What do you do when there is nothing to do? Did you like the last job better when it was busy or slow? Why? What other duties did you have?

A few tips on the interview itself:

- Be as interactive as possible. It's an audition, after all. Use plenty of what-if situations and have applicants demonstrate skills.
- Have key employees sit in on interviews and give feedback. What did they see? Would they want this person on their team?
- Have key employees give applicants a brief tour of the restaurant and talk about some specifics of the job. This time can be used to get a better gauge of applicants in an informal setting.
- Invite applicants to have a meal in the restaurant and, afterward, conduct a detailed assessment to see how observant they are about their experience.
- Don't hire applicants who have to be sold on taking the job. You shouldn't have to sell to them, they should be marketing their skills to you.
- Follow all legal requirements for interviewing and give everyone a chance.

The crew should be a reflection of your guest base, not carbon copies of you. A football team with 11 quarterbacks wouldn't be very successful. Fill the needs of the team. Keep in mind, too, that outgoing performers on-stage are often the quiet ones off-stage.

Don't get too caught up with the application itself. It's two-dimensional. Applicants are three-dimensional. And, bottom line, guests don't care about applications. They do care about being served by outstanding people with personality and sizzle. Interview, audition and role-play — then select the best.

Once your superstars are on-board, it's time to gear them up to provide *Quick Service That Sells!* It begins at orientation. Many of you may be thinking, "Yuck — orientation!" Is your orientation a 90-minute "policy-a-thon" consisting of the following items?

Typical Orientation

- Listen to a monologue from an unenthusiastic manager.
- Paperwork, paperwork, paperwork.
- Read the mission statement (which means little to new employees).
- Sit down with a long, boring handbook.
- Endless policies and procedures.
- Find out all the things you can and cannot do.
- Any questions? (Of course not, they're still too intimidated.)

Sounds like a trip to the principal, not a "Welcome to the team!"

Quick Service That Sells! Orientation

- Fun, upbeat welcome and introduction to the crew — it's the first day of a new career!
- Review benefits, payroll, schedules, training program, etc.
- Start on a high note — all the great things about working at the restaurant.
- Cover history, positions, common terms and a bit on profitability (so they understand where all the money goes).
- Take a thorough store tour, leading a "walking classroom." (In other words, don't plant new hires in a booth or leave them alone for 20 minutes to watch a video.)
- Review employee responsibilities (uniform, parking, guidelines).
- Cover the *Quick Service That Sells!* philosophy and employees' roles in the success of the business. (If this topic is not covered on Day One, it will be perceived as unimportant.)

> *Now That's* Quick Service That Sells!

Sizzle employees and they'll sizzle guests. To ensure consistent orientations, create color slides or flipcharts for managers to use and new hires to follow along. Whenever possible, involve star employees. They can lead tours, provide insights into the training program and talk about what it's like to work at the restaurant. Employees listen to peers more than managers. Establish a partner for new hires to go to with questions they may not want to ask superiors.

Orientations set the tone for the whole employment experience. Make yours interactive, seeking two-way communication every step of the way. A week or two afterward, conduct a "post-training orientation," during which you can find out if new hires have any questions now that they've been around a while. You can also solicit feedback about their training experience to date.

Next step, training. Airlines spend 14 hours of maintenance for every one hour of flying time. Are employees so lucky? Or is it, "Oh, great, another week of wearing a stupid 'trainee' nametag and shadowing another employee who really doesn't want to help or even know what he or she is doing."

Lose the trainee nametags. **Guests don't care if an employee is new. They just want outstanding service.** If guests were asked to rate a training program, how would they view its effectiveness? Solely based on the service they received.

Focus your training efforts on the items of importance to guests. Train on hospitality, not just tasks. Small details and nuances can be taught over time. Don't cram so much information into trainees' heads that they lose sight of what really matters or forget everything they've learned. Watch kids learn how to play a computer game. They don't read the manual, they figure it out by practicing and asking questions when needed. People learn differently so vary the methods — a mix of manuals, videos, job shadows, quizzes, skill assessments, role plays and plenty of practice!

Training typically is thought of like school. Schools educate you. Education is providing knowledge and information. Guests don't care about knowledge and information unless it translates into action. Training focuses on skills and behaviors.

Think about learning to drive. Step one is education (class, video, reading, tests) followed by training (on-the-road practice). A qualified instructor runs the show until the driver proves he or she is ready. The final leg is a demonstration of ability and a written test to obtain the coveted license. Are restaurant employees trained in this fashion? The downside to driver's ed? Everyone is treated the same way, no matter what their experience. Just as you need to customize the guest experience, you also need to customize the training experience.

Today's employees live in a digital world. They have been hit from all angles since the day they were born. They watch TV (the news channel with video, weather, sports scores and stock prices all on the same screen at once). At the same time, they can have an online chat (or six), listen to the stereo, talk on their cell phone, play a video game and do their homework all at the same time. VHS? Boring.

Think **T.O.D.**

Training **O**n **D**emand.

Give employees what they need to know right now. Later, give them what they need to know then. They function like DVD, skipping around to see only the parts they want to see at a given time.

Have a large menu? Train the top 20 items guests order (it's probably more than 80 percent of your sales). Ensure employees know those 20 items forward and backward. Follow up over the next few weeks to ensure they learn the remaining items as well.

Set up your training in "buckets" — three to 10 minutes long — covering only those items needed at that point. Don't subject employees to the whole program just because "it's the program."

Typical Training Program

- Read a boring manual, sit in a two-hour class or watch a long video.
- Cram tons of information into a short window of time.
- Focus on mechanics and steps.
- Get sent home early when it's slow to save labor.
- Follow someone around who may or may not follow standards.
- Pore over every last detail, even if it doesn't matter to guests.
- Memorize a bunch of stuff to pass a test (then forget it).
- Jump too quickly into a position and sink (LSD — Labor Saving Device — then get chalked up as a bad hire).
- Training, what's that?

Sound familiar? If so, here are a few suggestions:

Quick Service That Sells! Training Program

- Participate in rapid-fire changing of methods — small manuals or cards with bulleted information and lots of photos intermixed with role-plays, short classes and bursts of video for the initial portion of the day.
- Apply what was just learned by practicing as long as necessary.
- Enjoy a self-paced learning environment, moving on to the next step only after "getting" the previous one.
- Focus on hospitality and soft-skills — how you say things, body language and providing outstanding service to guests — role-play on the trainer, not the guest!
- Complete daily reviews and skill assessments, which also ensure trainers are on track.
- Work with trainers who have been validated to train and follow standards.

- Learn the main components of guest service and the job first, including key menu items. The rest will come down the road.
- Expect 30/90/180-day re-validations of skill and knowledge.

> *Now **That's** Quick Service That Sells!*

So how do trainers get selected and prepared? What process do they go through to get certified? If their only frame of reference is how they were trained, they may not be equipped to succeed and the cycle of training shortcomings will continue.

Try this exercise at your next trainer's meeting. Ask for a volunteer, then set the scene: "A barefoot alien has landed in the yard and desperately needs a pair of shoes. I'll pretend I'm the alien and, not knowing a thing about putting on and lacing up shoes, I'm going to follow your instructions exactly."

The volunteer may have no idea of where to start or where to go. Others in the group may pitch in an idea or two. Whatever the instruction, it's bound to be clumsy. You've tied your shoes thousands of times, but teaching another person to do it is difficult.

What matters? Getting the shoes tied. Yet folks involved in this exercise will often disagree about the "right way" to proceed. The point is that there are many right ways to tie shoes. Don't argue about how to get there — just focus on the end result.

Trainers need to be certified in the same fashion as new employees. Candidates should shadow a certified trainer in action, watching how he or she trains each topic, asking questions to reinforce information, and "lengthening the leash" to let the trainee gradually take on more responsibility, even in the face of a mistake or two. That's how people learn.

Typical Trainer Certification

- "You're my best employee — now you're a trainer. Get busy."
- "You've been here six months — now you're a trainer."
- "The trainer called in sick. Go train the new person." ("But I've only been here a week!")
- "Go to this class (or read this manual) and you will be certified."
- "I know you don't do it that way, but it's what the book says, so show them the right way."
- "The new employee has to be in full uniform, so do you."
- "Just let them follow you around and show them everything you do."
- "Do it because it's what the book says."
- "Training is *somebody else's* responsibility."

Quick Service That Sells! Trainer Certification

- Qualified candidates are given assignments to test ability and commitment. Example: They could create a small training module to reinforce cashier's menu knowledge.
- They learn how to deliver feedback and coach employees, using available resources (classes, books, videos) and role-plays to gain comfort with the process.
- They shadow an existing trainer to see how it's done.
- They learn the ins and outs of "classroom" training, starting with short classes such as menu knowledge, service delivery and register procedures. The 'classroom' may be a booth in the dining room. Limit distractions so the material and knowledge is transferred.
- A leader's guide or daily checklist of activities for the trainer to cover.
- They understand the "why" behind the standards and can explain them to trainees.

- They learn to monitor the success of new employees long after initial training is complete.
- "Training is *everyone's* responsibility."

> *Now That's* Quick Service That Sells!

Once there's a certified training team in place, managers need to validate the skills of new employees:

Typical Skill Validation

- "What's a skill validation? They passed the test — they're ready."
- "You know how to suggestively sell, don't you?"
- "You know how to greet the guest, right?"
- "You were trained in all these areas, right?"
- "Did you read the manual?"
- "Did you watch the video?"

Quick Service That Sells! Skill Validation

- There's a checklist of skills to assess.
- New employees demonstrate the appropriate skills to do their job.
- Manager provides feedback — not just saying what they did right, but finding out how they think they did versus what they wanted to do during each skill validation. Finally, what would they do differently next time? Ensure the trainee is ready to serve your guests.
- Action plan is developed to follow up on additional training needs.
- Trainers also receive feedback on their performance.

> *Now That's* Quick Service That Sells!

Hire me, train me, reward me, retain me. Two parts down. The crew has been hired and trained. Now they're taking care of guests — or are they? And what about existing crew?

chapter ten

Leading the Revolution

Treat employees like all-stars
**and they will treat the
consumer like a guest star.**

Training new employees is the simple part of the equation. In fact, opening a new restaurant — from a training perspective, at least — is ideal. There are no unwanted habits, preconceived notions or bad apples.

For most managers, however, there's an existing base of employees that need to be re-energized, re-focused and re-trained. Is it *re-diculous*? How do you get them to buy in to the new way? They've heard it all before. Most ignore it and, a few days later, it's back to business as usual.

The first step in convincing employees to embrace change is to describe the benefits. Try these two on for size: In the short-term, their enhanced service will drive other rewards (discussed further in Chapter 13). Long-term, it will build guest frequency, providing more hours for employees. But how does the new way get implemented?

Typical Implementation

- Manager schedules a mandatory meeting.
- Manager delivers a long monologue on why to deliver better service.
- Employees nod their heads in agreement.
- Lots of short-term rah-rah that wears off faster than a sugar-rush.
- Nothing changes.
- Manager gives up (stupid book — doesn't work in the real world!).

Quick Service That Sells! Implementation

- Manager solicits input from employees: What are we doing well? What needs to improve? How can better service be provided? Here are a few ideas we are considering, what do you think about them? What makes the job more difficult? What are guests saying? What prevents this from being a reality?
- Manager selects two to three employees to test the new procedures, including greetings, identifying why guests are visiting, situational selling, and so on.
- Manager schedules a *Fun-draising Rally*: "Learn how to make more money, get more hours and take care of more happy guests." (The very language used in the announcement is put into employee-benefiting terms.)
- At the rally, the manager introduces actual guests who describe how much they appreciate the new level of service. They visit more frequently.
- Employees who were the "test" describe how simple the new way is to do and how much better the service is.
- Manager introduces the first few components to focus on (identifying regulars as opposed to first-timers) and begins the process.

- Skeptical employees give it a try. Low and behold, it works (or they work elsewhere)!
- Managers continue to talk about it daily and gradually add more items into the mix.

Now That's Quick Service That Sells!

The focus group is critical. It shows that managers are listening, willing to hear input, and ready to address obstacles that surface during the testing phase of implementation. This test involves a small group of employees, who, in turn, contribute suggestions to enhance the process. Once actual implementation begins, other employees see "their own people" are proponents and it's not another program driven from the top down.

Prize the input you receive along the way. Respond accordingly, make enhancements as necessary, and propose solutions — don't just point out problems. As legendary baseball manager Casey Stengel said, "Managing is getting paid for home runs somebody else hits."

Approach the job as any sports team or professional band does: **Conduct a "draft" or "tryouts" (to find talent),** practice all the plays or music (training), cut the people who cannot perform (or re-direct them to new positions or employment), then play.

In the back of the house, managers oversee production. It's pretty black and white: What are the cook times? Are the recipes and portions followed? Is the order to standard? Are proper sanitation and safety procedures followed?

Managing service, however, is a little more subjective. Out front, you have to manage processes and perceptions, which differ among guests. Difficult, yes. Impossible, hardly!

Coaching *Quick Service That Sells!* can be easy. Choosing not to coach it is also easy. It's your choice. But you'll produce the best results when the employee behaviors you're after are repeated time after time. So coach the team daily, especially during the uncomfortable period of new-training implementation. The reward is worth it!

Be flexible, too. Providing outstanding service and hospitality is like a playground at recess. It may seem like chaos, but, in reality, teachers have established the parameters — no pushing, don't go past the edge of the playground, etc. The kids have flexibility and, more important, *fun* within those confines.

> Instead of mandating a set way to do every single thing in your restaurant, set ground rules as well as non-negotiable items, then allow employees to use their own style within those confines. You'll quickly see your top performers emerge, the ones who other employees look up to and want to work with.

Whatever you do, don't resort to nagging about every minute detail on how service is being delivered. If they are within the parameters, let them add their own personality. Otherwise, you'll end up creating mindless robots and take the fun out of the environment for the employees and the guests.

The non-negotiable items are service standards ...

> Standards that define and reinforce a culture of excellence. For example: The maximum time at the drive-thru window is 45 seconds or calls must be answered within three rings. These rules cannot be broken, but you can still allow flexibility by not specifying exactly what must be said to guests. In turn, this opens the door for situational selling to occur.

When you impose too many standards, employees get bored, guests feel processed and service suffers. Don't lower standards, but do focus on what really matters to guests (eliminate those that don't matter or allow flexibility about how it gets completed). If they don't care, don't worry about how it is specifically done. If they do care, get on it!

This is your environment. Make the most of it. The old saying — "Expectations determine results" — is true. If managers send out the message that the restaurant won't be busy or a new menu item won't sell, they'll be right. Failure is addictive. Managers who walk into the restaurant dragging their butt and lacking enthusiasm will soon have a whole crew treating guests the same way. On the other hand, if managers believe the crew can set sales, profit or service records, they'll reach loftier heights than managers who have low expectations.

> Success is also addictive — pass it on!

Before and during the shift, challenge your employees to set goals and track their performance. The best managers keep score, putting systems in place to show everyone where they stand. Examples: Run tracking reports or product-mix reports, then post them on the expo line or near the POS terminal. In the back of the house, use timers to track cook times or drive-thru times, then attach a score sheet or food cost reports to the time card or pay stub.

Employees may believe they're doing an outstanding job until they see how others are performing. This brand of coaching or mentorship ensures that employees are accountable to someone in addition to themselves. That's why people who work out with personal trainers or a friend achieve better results — they don't want to let the other person down. Reward progress and improvement.

Managers have the ability to walk right into the middle of the action, seeing and hearing what's happening and making necessary adjustments. But if they're so focused on a single task at hand (comping a complaint, for instance), they'll end up missing everything going on around them, compromising their ability to coach performances.

> Another shortcoming tends to occur when employees fall short of standards or expectations. Typical managers do one of two things:

1 Ignore it and thus communicate to everyone else that it's OK.

2 Drop the hammer on the person.

If managers dwell on the negative, **employees will start believing what they're hearing** and eventually create their own demise. An abundance of positive feedback, on the other hand, will swing the pendulum in the other direction, and performances will get better.

To gauge how crew perceives management, walk through the kitchen, look at an item and ask: "Who made this?" If employees look the other way or ask "What's wrong?" or point the finger at someone else, they're expecting something negative to come out of your mouth. Follow up with: "This is what I'm talking about! Everyone take a look at this burger — all our burgers should look this good."

On occasions when you do need to take corrective action, **order an "AND Sandwich."** For example: "Great job getting here on time *and* customers will appreciate it more if you're in full uniform. Get out there and do some great selling!" In other words, wrap two positives around the item to be corrected, and make sure you use the word "and" instead of "but." Also try to avoid using "you." Employees tend to take it as a personal attack on them and lose sight of the behavior needing to be changed. That method is like getting pulled over by the police. The driver broke a law, but is mad at the officer for catching them (when in reality, the driver made the mistake).

Typical Manager Feedback

- "Who made this — it looks terrible."
- "Sara, your area is filthy."
- "Get those drinks refilled."
- "What's your problem tonight?"
- "Smile, dammit!"
- "What did you do wrong now?"

Quick Service That Sells! Feedback

- "Outstanding uniform — **and** it'll be even more impressive if you arrive at your scheduled time. Is there anything I can do to help?"
- "Great job suggesting the larger-size value meals as we discussed!"
- "How can I help get the product to look like the last one?"
- "Thanks for coming in on time today. We talked about it yesterday and I appreciate you making the effort."

Now _That's_ Quick Service That Sells!

Take notice of how the previous feedback focused on "What can I do to help?" versus "What you did wrong." It's all about improving performance without sacrificing the respect of your employees. But if someone cannot or will not change, it's time to bring in qualified replacements.

Employees who don't have the talent or desire to deliver *Quick Service That Sells!* need to be given a fair shot to work in a place where service of this caliber isn't expected. Hopefully, at a competing restaurant. They'll fit right in.

When implementing the new service strategy, some employees will:

 Have no problem whatsoever adapting (the superstar).

 A larger percentage will perform inconsistently but have the potential to become stars (the B player).

 A few others may simply refuse to do a thing you ask. Don't get too caught up trying to whip the minority into shape.

We've all heard of the 80/20 rule: Your superstars generate the most sales and profits. Not quite sure if it's so dramatic in the restaurant industry, but the key is the "B" player. This group typically makes up about 50 percent of your crew. To run your restaurant successfully, you need to have the B players improving their performance. They can do the job, but don't always seem to perform at a high enough level.

Each day they arrive, they ask: "Who's closing tonight?" If a manager who expects little is on duty, this group gives little. If the manager on duty is one who has high standards, demands plenty but rewards and recognizes, these employees perform at the higher level. Ultimately, it's the guests who benefit. Incentivize the B player and you'll have 75 percent to 80 percent of your employees doing exactly what you want — delivering outstanding service. The others? Time to go elsewhere!

To get maximum impact in your operation, rank employees — one, two, three, etc. — in each key position. On busy shifts, align the top talent with the key sales positions. If drive-thru is 65 percent of your business, should the best cashier be stationed there (along with your top production crew)? For a delivery/

carryout operation, have your top phone reps working the peak time — you make or lose the most money during this time. It's much like an orchestra. If the first-chair performer isn't available, put in the second chair, not the fourth. The job simply becomes conducting the performance, knowing full well that one sour note could lead to ruin or "just another concert" for guests.

Set the energy level high and maintain it — be a thermostat. Keep standards high and demand excellence. In return, reward performance, appreciate efforts to change and improve, and more will follow. After all, employees demand excellence in the person who controls the action and sets the tone — the manager!

Coaching on Game Day

Got it **just don't get it.**

Outkast — 'Hey Ya'

It's action-packed two or three shifts per day depending on hours of operation. There's a tendency for managers to roll up their sleeves to get through the day. After all, managers set the pace. How upbeat is the shift going to be today? What's today's focus? Employees responding with a "got it" to the manager but not demonstrating the item won't "get it." Do you really believe they are providing the desired level of service if you have never seen them demonstrate it?

As a manager, it's important to see things from an "aerial view." What's the big picture? How can the team get there? Where are we today? What needs to change to make tomorrow's shift better? How can time be spent to make guests' experiences really sizzle? Work on the business, not just in it.

As the assessment takes place, prioritize what needs to be done, working backward from the "perfect visit" to reach goals as quickly as possible. Implement and engrain behaviors on the two or three key items that will make the biggest impact on guests. Then focus on the next three and so on.

Evaluate the restaurant, employees and guests. What should guests' experiences look like? What is a perfect visit? Do employees know what it looks like? Start high — with the management team. Does each manager set the example? Model the behaviors?

To close the gap and move toward service excellence, enlist the help of the crew to envision and write down what constitutes the perfect visit. Start outside the restaurant and describe what guests should see, feel and experience at each sizzle point. Post it for employees to see, highlighting each position's piece of the puzzle.

Run your shifts along the same route guests take, staying one step ahead of the action at all times. Address anything not up to the standard of the perfect visit.

Many restaurant companies initiate "walking paths" or "loops" to check on business. But **if managers focus so intently on the step they're supposed to be doing, they'll** tune out **all other things going on around them.**

In those instances, guests become invisible. And, pretty soon, the whole crew will follow suit, oblivious to guest's needs — the empty ice machine at the beverage bar, dirty condiment holders or a filthy drive-thru lane. It all becomes part of the scenery.

Great managers take "shift vital signs" as they work the restaurant. Others simply walk the path because it's scheduled at a certain time of day. Like any other process or tool, it's only as effective as the person conducting the check.

Typical Pulse Check

- Start near the register and look around.
- Walk through the dining room.
- Go into the kitchen. Everything *looks* fine (from a distance).
- Grab a cup of coffee and feel good that nobody complained: "I run a great shift!"

What did the check miss? Dirty, sticky tables, no proper greetings or situational selling, dirty restrooms, drive-thru cashier needs change, cook times high, three guests ignored as you walked by. At least you did the loop.

Watch out, however. Employees are a product of their environment. They'll mimic the behaviors they see on the floor. If managers slip on sizzle, so will the crew.

Quick Service That Sells! Pulse Check — Quick-Serve/Fast-Casual

- Walk outside to check the micro-trash, front doors and entry and, in the process, thank any departing guests and welcome those arriving. Check the drive-thru path if applicable. As you move inside, you:
- Move into the dining room, visit some tables and interact with guests. Tables need busing? Pre-busing? Spills to clean?
- Check the beverage and/or condiment area. Clean? Restock necessary? Interact with any guests in the area.
- A quick detour to the restroom to ensure it's spotless (send someone to check on the restroom of the opposite sex).
- Stop, look and listen to the cashiers. Change, cups or supplies needed? Properly greeting guests? Situational selling? Explaining service sequence to first-time guests? Coach and praise the cashier team.
- Drive-thru times quick? Listen to greeting, situational selling and ensure attendant is repeating the order as the food is handed to the guest. Recognize great performance.

- Then it's on to the kitchen. Cook times and quality exceeding standard? Prep levels fine? Additional items needed? Thank the kitchen crew for a job well-done!

- A few pats on the back for a great shift and it's time to check sales.

- Run a sales report. Are you ahead of projection? Slow? Do you need to cut labor or get the cashiers to situationally sell even better to meet the day's goal?

> *Now **That's*** Quick Service That Sells!

Quick Service That Sells! Pulse Check — Delivery/Carryout

- Walk outside to check the micro-trash, front doors and entry and, in the process, thank any departing guests and welcome those arriving. As you move inside, you:

- Check lobby and/or dining area. Clean? Doors and windows clean and streak free? How are guests being greeted?

- Phone. Listen! Proper greeting, situational selling, repeating order and thanking guests? Hold time? Answered quickly? Need additional crew?

- If applicable, a quick detour to the restroom to ensure it's spotless (sending someone to check on the restroom of the opposite sex).

- Stop, look and listen to the cashiers. Change, boxes or supplies needed? Properly greeting guests? Double-checking the carryout orders with each guest? Coach and praise the cashier team.

- Then it's on to the kitchen. Cook times and quality exceeding standard? Prep levels fine? Additional items needed? Thank the kitchen crew for a job well-done!

- A few pats on the back for a great shift and it's time to check sales.
- Run a sales report. Are you ahead of projection? Slow? Do you need to cut labor or get the phone reps to situationally sell even better to meet the day's goal?

Now That's Quick Service That Sells!

Hands-On Management Ensures Success (H.O.M.E.S.)

In the previous examples of the Typical Pulse Check versus the **Quick Service That Sells!** Pulse Check, both managers followed a similar path yet produced dramatically different results. Typical managers merely go through the motions, not paying enough attention to their surroundings. Astute managers have keen restaurant senses, hearing buzzers going off, sensing empty ice machines, seeing things no ordinary human can. They uncover and fix problems before guests become aware that anything was even wrong.

Break down your own loop, adding an action step at every stop. Examples:

- "Check the front door" becomes "Open the door and welcome guests."
- "Check the register" becomes "Ring up an order" (and listen to the other cashiers).
- "Check the dining room" becomes "Visit first-time guests and introduce yourself."

Focus on four to five quick-hit items to look for while going through the action steps previously described. Your process of checking needs to be hands-on, not just visual. Can you really tell if some things are done properly without up-close inspection? A sticky table, after all, looks fine from a distance (but not to the guest sitting there).

Here's an example of what your detailed Pulse Check with action steps may look like:

1) Open the door and welcome arriving guests/thank departing guests.

- Micro-trash check (out to first row of cars).
- Glass and brass clean?
- Floors clean and dry?
- Great first impressions for arriving guests?

2) Ring up an order.

- Cashiers need change?
- Situational selling?
- Explaining the service sequence if needed?
- Recognize a cashier for something outstanding.

3) Make an order in the kitchen

- Cook times.
- Product quality.
- Prep levels.
- Cleanliness.

4) Take a drive-thru order.

- Drive-thru times at/exceed standard.
- Situational selling; condiment requests at speaker box.
- Delivering hospitality.
- Change and drinks ready.
- Describing order as it's handed to guest.

5) Deliver food to a guest (or page them to pick-up).

- Describe food to guest.
- Thank guest. Provide condiments or direct to condiment/beverage bar.
- Cook times to standard?
- Employees providing outstanding service?

6) Check the restroom (and send someone of the opposite sex to the other one).

- Floors clean, debris-free and dry?
- Mirrors and sinks clean and dry?
- Toilet paper/paper towels stocked?
- Restroom checks being done by crew?
- Check stalls and/or urinals.
- Wash hands.

7) Check on a guest.

- Food outstanding?
- Why are they visiting?
- Get their names.
- Invite them back.
- Deliver a free dessert sample or appetizer sample to an unsuspecting guest.

8) Check the beverage and/or condiment bar (if applicable)

- Refills needed?
- Clean and wiped down?
- All supplies well-stocked.
- Interact with a guest.
- Praise/coach employee responsible for the area.

9) Take a cleanliness lap around the building.

- Parking Lot.
- Landscaping.
- Drive-thru lane (if applicable).
- Menu, preview boards and signage.
- Windows, doors, glass and floors.

10) Run sales and product mix reports.

- Sales meeting projection?
- Product mix — modify any prep items as needed.
- Communicate with the team — sales needs, running low on items, suggest a specific item, thank crew for exceeding goals.
- Make necessary labor adjustments.

11) Recognize an employee — one per hour (minimum).

- 30-second review: What is working? What is making their job difficult? How can I help?
- Praise something they did right.

At one point or another, virtually every manager has tried to run a restaurant by him or herself. Can't be done, can it? You end up missing things, even running the pulse check every hour.

Teach employees and other managers to think. Teach them to see what you see. Teach them to look for what you're looking for. If there are items below standard, deliver feedback that teaches employees or managers to think and act. The more the employees see and do, the more time you can spend talking to guests and hearing how well you are doing!

Typical Manager

"How come you haven't maintained those tables?"

"Why didn't you suggestive sell?"

Nag, nag, nag.

Quick Service That Sells! Manager

"Let's go through the five key points in your area — what do you see we're doing right?" (Deliver appropriate praise.)

"Now, what needs attention?"

If employees don't see the things you're looking for, give clues.

Offer solutions or assistance. Ask what they can do differently next time to avoid those situations.

Now That's Quick Service That Sells!

Encourage employees to do a mini-pulse check in their area along with some common areas and, pretty soon, they'll be truly zeroing in on what delights guests. Develop a list of responsibilities for everyone — no matter what section they're in, what position they hold or who they are.

Some areas to consider "everyone's responsibility"

Arriving Guests

The Hospitality Zone

Restrooms

Refills

Table Maintenance

Arriving Guests. Greet incoming guests before they get to the register. Eye contact and a smile also help set a positive, comforting tone. "Welcome!"

The Hospitality Zone. Employees make eye contact with any guest who approaches within three to four steps and verbally acknowledges any guest who gets within one to two steps. In the dining room, crew can say "hello" and "welcome" to the newly arrived. If employees aren't interacting with guests, a few sizzle points just fizzled. Crew should also take notice of puzzled or frustrated looks — guests waiting for their order, to place an order, to pay the check, or needing a drink refill, etc. Take care of those needs or get someone who can!

Restrooms. Yes, someone is ultimately responsible for them, but if an employee is in there, he or she can pick up the paper towels on the floor, flush the toilets and urinals, and wipe down the sinks (and wash hands afterward). Guests don't deserve to walk into a filthy restroom.

Refills. Offer drink refills. It's not expected, but certainly welcomed — it sizzles!

Table maintenance. Whenever an employee walks through the dining room, he or she should remove unwanted items.

Guests deserve personal attention from every employee. After all, they're doing the restaurant a favor by dining there. When the entire team pitches in, it shows guests that they're the top priority.

Appendix C contains a small card (also available in a downloadable file at www.pencominternational.com) to carry around and use when doing pulse checks in your restaurant. Stop, look, listen and coach — make it an hourly routine as you work the room. When you're alert, there are many things you'll see and be able to improve.

Reinforcing the Message

It's 11 a.m. (or 5 p.m.) —
**do you know how your
guests are being cared for?**

Somewhere between initial training and today, a percentage of employees' knowledge and skill is lost. How much or how little depends on the frequency of practice and reinforcement. Guests, meanwhile, don't care about the past. They're interested in the service they're receiving at the present time. Are you confident your employees can deliver?

Try a little word association, having crew members write down three things that pop into their minds when they hear each of the following terms. *Don't spell the words, only say them.* Once employees are done, they should compare lists with a partner to observe the number of matches.

 See Appendix D for common words associated with these terms.

Word Association

Run _____

Sell _____

Sale _____

Buy _____

Strike _____

Fall _____

Set _____

Fair _____

Out of the 24 possible answers, chances are most people matched fewer than six (25 percent). This list has eight well-known words, but, by not spelling them out, employees may hear something different than intended ("cell" versus "sell," for instance). In addition, many of these words have multiple meanings. "Set" has more than 460 and "run" more than 390!

Suggestive Selling Mistakes

Why conduct this exercise? People often assume everyone is thinking or interpreting words the same way. Managers ask cashiers or phone reps to "suggestively sell." What does that mean? A few of their sales lines may be:

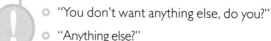

- "You don't want anything else, do you?"
- "Anything else?"
- "If I don't ask, we lose points on the mystery shop."

These are all examples (albeit weak ones) of suggestive selling and undoubtedly have been heard at one time or another, maybe in your own restaurant. Telling a cashier to "greet the guest" could be interpreted as:

Greeting Mistakes

- "Next!"
- "Can I take your order?"
- "Ready to order?"
- "For here or to go?"
- Blank stare waiting for the guest to order.

Again, all of these examples fit the definition of "greet," but they don't sizzle. It's like asking kids if they cleaned their rooms. Is their definition of "clean" the same as the parents'?

By the end of this book, you may know how to deliver *Quick Service That Sells!* But ask yourself: Are employees on the same wavelength? The more you talk about service, the more focused and adept you'll become at raising the bar of excellence for your guests. Ideas are the easy part, daily execution by every employee will make the difference!

Here are a few easy-to-implement tools and tips to ensure employees get their daily dose of *Quick Service That Sells!*

Pre-Shift Meeting. Also known as the huddle, Alley Rally and other things, the pre-shift meeting is nothing new, but is it even being done in your operation? Do you conduct one? Is it effective? Is it done properly? Is this your definition of a pre-shift meeting?

Typical Pre-Shift Meeting

- One-sided monologue led by the managers.
- Manager drones on about useless information or harps on things going wrong, sucking the energy out of employees.
- Managers ask questions that yield little, so they can check off the "conduct pre-shift meeting" box on their daily checklist. For example, "Do you know the new menu items we have?" "Can you suggestively sell value meals?" "Does everyone know how to upsell?"
- Employees nod their head "yes" each time managers ask a question such as the ones above.
- Nothing changes (including the downward sales spiral).

Quick Service That Sells! Pre-Shift Meeting

- Two-way dialogue between managers and employees.
- Manager asks questions, but with different results:
  - "John, describe your favorite combo meal."
  - "Sue, a guest orders it. What is your response?"
  - "Courtney, I order a large sausage pizza. What is your response?"
  - "Matthew, how many are you going to sell tonight? How much is the value meal?"
  - "Leticia, I didn't order a dessert, what would you say?"
  - "Todd, I've never been here before, what would you recommend?"
  - "Jane, I call and say I have to order for 20 people. What would you suggest I order?"
- Manager reviews an item of the day and allows everyone to have a small taste.
- Cashiers are asked to set personal goals for the shift (ticket average, sales of specific items, etc.).
- The guest experience and sales *rock!*

Now That's Quick Service That Sells!

The little voice inside you may be saying: "But in my store, we can't do a pre-shift meeting all at one time and get everyone together." There are two options: 1) Don't conduct the pre-shift meeting (like many of your competitors) and hope everything goes well, or 2) figure out a way to review the key items just mentioned. It's easiest to conduct the meetings at one time (keep them very short), but if scheduling requires flexibility, schedule them at 30-minute intervals (5:00, 5:30 and 6:00).

Remember **T.O.D.**

Training **O**n **D**emand.

If the interval system won't work, spend a short time with each employee as he or she arrives. As you go over the information in the style previously described, take the opportunity to review appearance standards and deliver praise whenever possible. A leading fast-casual chain calls it TIP/TOP.

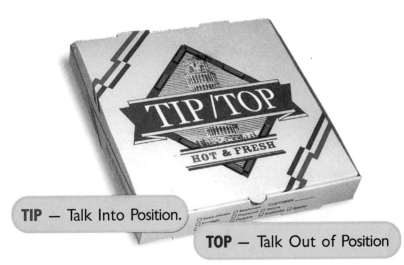

TIP — Talk Into Position.

TOP — Talk Out of Position

TIP — Talk Into Position. Spend 30 to 60 seconds role-playing with one or a small group of employees. Ask questions so the employees are reciting the information versus hearing it from the manager. Provide praise and suggestions as necessary. Set goals with the employees to ensure they maximize their potential. Thirty seconds apiece for five employees — that's 150 seconds or two minutes of a manager's time. It's a great way to set the tone and pace of the shift.

TOP — Talk Out of Position. Spend 30 seconds as employees are getting ready to leave. Review your observations, sales numbers or other relevant information. What worked well during the shift? What opportunity is there to improve next shift? Any guest suggestions? Did employees hit their sales goals discussed during the TIP? Provide plenty of feedback and recognition. Why would any of the employees want to find a new job if they receive a mini-appraisal and an opportunity to provide input each and every day?

Now That's Quick Service That Sells!

Still worried your pre-shift meetings will be drab? Think back to your school days for a minute. Multiple-choice tests seemed easier than other forms of testing, didn't they? You could figure out an answer from the list of possibilities. But was the information really understood? To succeed at fill-in-the-blank tests, on the other hand, you really had to know your stuff.

Lead your pre-shift meetings with a fill-in-the-blank approach. It's far more effective in helping employees retain information. Also be sure to infuse daily variety and change. Otherwise, the meetings can stagnate and bore employees.

Other meeting suggestions:

Use a whiteboard. Communicate daily promotions, featured items, focus of the day, etc., so employees can review it prior to hitting the floor.

Provide 3x5 shift cards. As employees arrive, they receive a card filled out by the manager on duty. It describes special assignments for the day, sales or greeting lines, desired food and beverage descriptions — all to be used as reference throughout the shift.

Recipe of the day. Select an item or three to review with the front-of-the-house crew. In the back of the house, have kitchen crew prepare the item exactly to standard. Cooks get to hone their preparation skills, cashiers/phone reps get to taste items which, in turn, they can describe to guests in better detail: "We tried one earlier today and it's outstanding!" Who can resist? One item per day and the menu will be completely trained in one or two months in a typical restaurant.

Around the dial. One by one, have front-of-the-house crew name a characteristic, price, or other information about a featured menu item. What's missing? Who provided the best descriptions? Managers don't have all the information — employees do. This exercise encourages employees to share best practices and hear from peers, not just the boss.

Trainer for a day. Assign a menu-item training for the day and let an employee lead that part of the pre-shift meeting. He or she will learn how to prepare a training message, ask effective questions, praise and re-direct, etc. With the manager nearby to provide assistance, employees can become more comfortable presenting in front of a group and may even lay the groundwork to become actual trainers down the road.

Reality TV. Assign a menu item or portion of the menu to small groups of employees. Have them prepare a short video or presentation for the next shift meeting. A twist on the old class favorite Show and Tell. When people teach, they learn. Did you notice a great cashier suggestion? Share these best practices at the next meeting. Videotape it so others not on duty can receive the benefit of seeing excellence in action.

Description prescription. A great way to jazz up pre-shift meetings is to have employees come up with unique descriptive words or phrases for their favorite menu items. Throw out a question to get it rolling and see who can come up with the most descriptive phrases. Post them in the break area or communication board so others can use the ideas.

Quote of the day. Post a quote about service, motivation or positive news each day. Employees are barraged with nothing but negative information in the papers and on TV. Post some good news or a funny quote to disconnect them from the negativity and put them into the proper frame of mind. Control the atmosphere. Success is contagious — pass it on!

Do I know you? Have employees write down one interesting fact about themselves, then list the facts on duplicated Bingo-style game boards and pass them out. During lulls in the shift, employees need to find out which person each of the facts describes. Once they complete the card, they win a prize. It's an effective way to promote teamwork and get to know each other.

Useless information challenge. To help your crew have something to talk about with guests in the dining room, select four to five different items to uncover about guests. Not only will it add variety to the shift and the experience, it creates fun interaction with the guests (far different from the competition). For example:

- Guest who drove the farthest distance to get here.
- Guest who drove the shortest distance.
- Guest celebrating the most senior birthday.
- Family with the most children.

Power cards. Create a series of cards — bound or kept in a small binder — that contain all the relevant information for menu items, or have descriptions and ingredients of popular desserts and appetizers. Employees can quiz each other (or the manager can lead quizzes) throughout the shift during slow times. For back-of-the-house employees, use the cards to review recipes and plate-presentation standards.

Guest trivia. Have cashiers ask guests (especially kids) a trivia question for the chance to win a discount or free item. Use questions from board games or have your own ("What is your favorite item?").

The restaurant landscape is filled with competitors who deliver ordinary experiences extraordinarily well. Shake things up. Try something new. Be different every day. Your delivery of interactive service will wow guests, sending them out the door wondering how great their next visit will be ... and it will be soon!

Training on demand, meanwhile, will keep employees on their toes, reinforcing communication, knowledge and service skills. It also fosters fun interaction with guests. And fun translates into great experiences.

chapter thirteen

Rallying the Troops

> **If you want to enhance the guest experience,** you have to improve the employee experience.
>
> — *TJ Schier*

To truly deliver outstanding service to every guest, every visit, the whole crew needs to be trained and ready to deliver. Employees are leery of managers who tell their employees "be nicer," "provide better service" and "work harder." All the while, the managers are treating them like mushrooms (keeping them in the dark and feeding them manure).

To maximize the effectiveness of change, demonstrate to employees how they'll benefit from the new service focus and treat them better. **The number one motivating factor** for employees is full appreciation of their efforts. If they currently give 95 percent and receive no positive feedback, why should they give 100 percent?

Incentives focus on two groups: the A players (who already deliver great service) and the B players (who have the ability but use it selectively). Incentives, contests and recognition help ensure the A players are motivated to continue doing what they do best and to get better at it. Unfortunately, they represent a small percentage of the employee base. The majority — the B player — is wondering: "Who's closing tonight?"

Of the two groups, B is the most important to the success of your restaurant. To perform at a high level, B players need someone or a system to hold them accountable. If nobody's keeping an eye on them or expecting great performance, they can slack with the best of them. Incentives, contests and recognition drive this group onward and upward.

> Not all incentives, contests and recognition, however, are created equal. Which would be more effective for a health club?

> **o** Work out 100 times in six months and receive a chance to win a cruise.

Or:

> o Work out 25 times — get a free T-shirt, 50 times — a free month's dues, 100 times — a $50 gift card.

Members could work out 100 times in the first example and still lose. They're in shape, which means they performed their end of the deal, but likely received zero incentive in return. In fact, many would have probably given up once they realized they had little chance of winning. In the second example, meanwhile, members scored numerous prizes.

The key to long-term success is setting intermediate benchmarks. Like the football team who gains 10 yards in four plays to keep going, incentives allow employees to celebrate small successes as they march on to larger ones. How the employees are treated through this process will determine their ability to stick with it. Managers are training partners, ensuring that employees show up every day for their workouts. Managers encourage, challenge and reward. But do managers know how?

A word on incentives:

Don't confuse them with a lottery. "Sell an item and be in the drawing for a trip" is not effective. Many people sell and someone is lucky enough to win. There is no correlation between the performance (how much someone sold) and winning.

Incentives are ideal to drive changes in behavior. Having a grand prize is great — it has sex appeal and keeps people motivated. However, there needs to be rewards for any employee who increases sales or performance levels. If not, he or she will do additional work and won't be rewarded for it.

Employee recognition isn't a program. It should be an integral part of the culture, where incentives and contests are tools used to mold behaviors and move the team to a higher level. Here are a number of ideas to help get the ball rolling:

FUN-D RAISER. Cashiers receive one point for every $1 in incremental sales they drive. First, determine and communicate the benchmark ticket average in your operation. If, at the end of the shift, an employee has served 100 guests with a ticket average a dollar higher than the benchmark, he or she would earn 100 points for the $100 in incremental sales generated. Points are saved up for prizes.

This contest also works well for selling specific items or lowering food costs. The key to success is utilizing the current benchmark (or historical average) and only rewarding performance exceeding it. The contest becomes self-funding because money is only paid out (in the form of prizes) when additional sales are generated (or costs lowered).

Keep in mind that this contest can work for selling specific items, but past experience has proven that selling more of one appetizer or dessert usually cannibalizes another so the net effect is zero. Allowing employees to focus on ticket average gives them the flexibility to use situational selling, as discussed earlier.

Employee Incentives and Contests

NAME GAME. Employees earn pins or prizes for learning a preset number of guests' names. This simple contest encourages interaction and underscores who pays the bills. A leading buffet chain rewards employees who learn 100 names. Ask employees to focus on getting and using guests' names during their visits. Everyone appreciates being called by name versus being treated like a number.

"GET TO KNOW ME" BINGO. To encourage employees to interact with guests in the dining room, create a bingo card containing various items for employees to uncover while running their shift. Examples could include: Guest wearing a red shirt, guest who plays tennis, guest who has more than two children, guest who works within two miles of the restaurant and so on. Employees will have to use their imagination and skills to discover the information. As they talk to guests, they "get the square" when they find a guest with the item they're looking for. Prizes are awarded for first bingo, completing all squares, etc.

CLOSEST TO THE PIN. Have cashiers or phone reps try to predict how many of a specific item they'll sell for the day. In the back of the house, kitchen crew can try to guess total food waste, number of remakes, busiest product hour or ideal food cost versus theoretical. A word of advice: Do a "farthest from the pin" (person who exceeds projection by the most) on items you are selling so employees don't sell a certain number and then stop selling to win the contest.

COOK (or DRIVE-THRU) TIME/QUALITY. Have a specified number of points, lottery tickets or tickets for a drawing available to the kitchen crew for the shift. Every time a product goes over the specified time or doesn't meet standards, points are deducted or tickets are lost. The crew divides up whatever remains at the end. Peer pressure is more effective than management pressure and it promotes teamwork and quality.

FIND THE DOT, CLEAN THE SPOT. Place date labels around those hard-to-clean places, including under the dish machine, behind equipment, under stacks of cups or boxes, etc. Basically, any place you need to clean. Employees find the dots, clean the spots and earn points and/or prizes.

WORLD RECORDS. Create a series of records to encourage productivity and competition. Simple tasks such as fastest production or prep times, safety records, test completion times, side duties completed and so on can make work fun.

What prizes should you hand out? Which are the best and most effective? Don't assume you know. Ask! Find out what makes employees tick. Learning what they do in their spare time will shed light on what rewards are ideal.

There are two great books to help you out: *Playing Games at Work: 52 Incentives, Contests and Rewards for the Hospitality Industry* ($19.95 from Pencom Press, call 800-247-8514 or visit www.pencominternational.com) and *Send Flowers to the Living! Rewards, Contests and Incentives to Build Employee Loyalty* ($16.95 from Incentivize Solutions, call 800-247-8514 or visit www.pencominternational.com).

Cut the custom deal. Employees want a choice of shifts? Fine, they need to run the highest ticket average. They want to be off early on Friday nights? Fine, they need to do certain side work. If they don't live up to their end of the bargain, the deal is off. Just don't forget to live up to your end.

Is it harder to manage this way? Seems like it, but it really isn't. The expectations are clearly set: **perform a certain way and receive an agreed upon** reward.

Many employees will see this as unfair. Unfair? Unfair is paying employees the same wages for far different productivity levels. Unfair is giving a 5 percent raise to the great employee and 3 percent to the average employee. Unfair is keeping the slackers around who don't produce. **Unfair is piling the extra work on the superstars.**

Fair is rewarding and compensating employees for the productivity they provide. Fair is having A players work the busy shifts, making the most of the opportunity. Reward your great performers. Get rid of your non-performers. That's fair!

Rewards don't have to be lavish. And how they're presented is as important as the reward itself. Insincere gifts from managers (or grumbling about how much prizes cost) won't mean as much or may even drive away employees quicker. Words of encouragement and praising are free and very meaningful. As the old saying goes: **"Well-done should come out of a manager's mouth more often than just talking about hamburgers."**

Cash tends to be a tempting incentive, but its effects wear off quickly. A 20-dollar bill for selling the most of an item will simply go into the employee's wallet or purse. There is no link between the performance and the reward. A $20 gift card presented in a company note card will drive home the connection. If cash is used, try $1 gold coins. Most employees will save them or at least remember where they came from if they get spent.

Remember, the key is to find out what excites employees and give it to them in the form of incentives. Employees, meanwhile, must get the job done in order to continue to receive the incentives. It's a performance agreement. If they fall short, the deal is off.

Here's how to appreciate your employees:

Thank them — verbally or with handwritten notes.

Listen to them — solicit input and suggestions. Reward cost-saving and sales-driving ideas.

Ask them to join an employee council to help recommend solutions to issues.

Allow them to write their own schedule for a week.

Provide additional development or training.

Offer recognition to distinguish employees from their peers as a motivator.

Give incentive pay — a dollar extra per hour. It's a great way to cover hard-to-fill shifts or stations.

Other winning ideas:

- Paid time off.
- Free meals.
- A pass allowing employees' family to come in for a free meal. Don't forget to stop by and visit them.
- "Get out of work free" card (15/30/60 minutes).
- "Get out of *side work* free" card.
- Free haircut, car wash, oil change or dry cleaning.
- Gift cards for video rentals, gas, other restaurants, electronic stores, etc.
- Movie pass — combined with paid time off for a big wow.
- Lottery tickets — where else could employees have a chance to retire immediately?
- Calling card.

- Picture on a "wall of fame" or "world records" board. Track highest sales, ticket average, lowest cook times, fastest prep times, most positive compliments, etc. People will do extraordinary things to set a record.

- Logoed hats and key chains.

- Pins. They're conversation starters with guests and set people apart.

- A 10-cent raise (it costs only $4 per week if recipients work 40 hours).

- Name a day or part of the office or restaurant after them.

PTD   **P**aid **T**o **D**o

AAB   **A**bove **A**nd **B**eyond

To create a culture of excellence, set high expectations and manage toward them every second. The following items are "PTDs" - items the employees are 'Paid To Do'. These are expectations and requirements of every employee. Employees not doing these basic things are either not expected to (i.e. a management issue) or were mis-cast in their role. YOU need to ensure these basics are happening. The following items are listed here to help you move performance forward in these areas if it is not already there. Once there, your focus needs to be on the items listed in the next section.

> **Showing up on time.** "Thanks for coming in on time today. I wish all employees focused on punctuality like you."
>
> **Doing what they're supposed to do.** "Great job portioning out the chicken."

Making improvements in areas they were weak in. "We talked last week about consistency and I wanted to thank you for the effort you have made in ensuring each taco looks exactly like the picture."

Uniform compliance. "Great job on the uniform today. Hey, everyone, take a look at how Jeff is dressed today. This is how it's done!"

Profitable suggestive selling. "Awesome job, Sally, suggesting the two-fer pizza special. I'd like to post the line you used with the guests in the break area if that's all right."

Product quality. "Who made this? Looks great! Let's see them all come out like this."

Production times. "Nice job in the kitchen with ticket times — it's really helping the drive-thru!"

Also make it a point to catch employees doing the right things:

> While it is nice to praise the 'PTDs,' it is much more effective to focus on, praise and celebrate efforts and results that are AAB (Above and Beyond) the set and expected cultural standards.

Positive guest comments. "Jenny, the guests who just ordered complimented how nice you were while taking their order. I really appreciate the effort — it's helping build sales and it makes my job much easier. Thanks!"

Top performance on a busy shift. "Way to go kitchen team — record sales and no mistakes! Performance like this ensures our cashiers, phone reps and drive-thru can focus on the guests. I really appreciate it!"

Budgets achieved/costs lowered. "John, thanks for the extra attention on minimizing waste over the last week. Our food cost went down 0.1 percent. Keep it up!"

Covering a shift or extra work. "I really appreciate you coming in early today to cover for the no-show. The guests are lucking out today being taken care of by you."

Great ideas. "Great suggestion to eliminate the bottle-neck at the expo line, Susie. Everyone will benefit."

Taking one for the team. "I know you didn't agree with the decision, but I really appreciate you supporting it during the shift."

A word of caution: Incentives can never get the wrong people to do the right things. If a sub-par employee is terminated who was working 40 hours per week at $8 per hour, the $320 can be used to provide raises — a 25-cent raise to 32 employees who work 40 hours per week. Or, better yet, a few large raises for great employees and moderate raises for those who are improving. The rest of the money can go toward rewards and incentive prizes.

You can't win every guest alone. Incentives, contests and rewards will help you get things done through your people. The restaurant wins when everyone works together toward common goals. The result? Sales, profits and retention levels rise while stress levels fall.

Now That's Quick Service That Sells!

chapter fourteen

Marketing

Marketing was placed toward the end of this book for a reason — get everything else done first. Far too many companies spend millions of dollars marketing an inferior product and average service. But if you promote a dud, guess what? More people will know it's a dud.

A more cost-effective approach is to implement the action steps prescribed in the chapters of this book. If you do, you'll create a word-of-mouth buzz driving free P.R. and valuable referrals.

Once your restaurant is running at the desired levels of service, you can unleash the marketing beast. Until then, it makes no sense to attract more guests into a restaurant that doesn't sizzle. In fact, many marketing ideas — clever ones, too — have bitten the dust because the service supporting them was merely average or OK.

The best sequence? Fix the product, make it outstanding, then market it. You can call on numerous marketing strategies such as TV commercials, radio advertising, remotes, coupons in the local paper, newspaper advertising — even an "Under New Management" banner. These *external* methods, however, aren't nearly as important as what you do *internally* to get guests to come back.

Take a moment to think about successful restaurants around your neighborhood. Which ones advertise? How do they do it? Many have built a very loyal guest base by providing tremendous service and by making everyone feel important ... like they're family ... like they're a name, not a number.

> **It's a fact:** Guests want to go where they're known.

And the easiest way to know them is to ask for their name, remember it, and use it whenever they visit. If appropriate, purchase a point-and-shoot camera to record the fun times guests have in your operation. Hang the photographs in a public place, honoring your regulars and attracting the attention of your newcomers.

Do whatever it takes to make guests feel special.

Take a sincere interest in their everyday lives, try to anticipate their needs, make them out to be the most important person in your store. After all, they're the reason you're in business. They'll also be extremely receptive to your external-marketing efforts, especially those designed to improve visit frequency.

Whatever time and money you decide to spend on these efforts, it's wise to invest an equal, if not greater amount, on ramping up your internal marketing — the quality of service your crew provides along with the marketing messages communicated to guests while they're in the house.

That's right — *in the house*. The mistake often made is to view a promotion as an end in itself. To be effective, however, you have to think beyond merely attracting guests in the door. You also have to encourage them to make purchases, enjoy the experience your employees provide and, most important, come back another day — all of which requires well-trained employees who can speak to the promotion and execute at the point of sale. Guests can't participate in the event if they don't know what's going on.

In planning a promotion, try to determine where you want to end up before you rush out of the gate. First, project the revenue you're likely to generate, then allocate a percentage of it to cover your costs — costs you've determined in advance. If you're after short-term success, be happy with nothing less than a 10-dollar return on every dollar invested.

If, for example, you've projected $5,000 in promotional revenue, the budget should be around $500 for the event itself. On the other hand, you could accept a four-to-one return if you can expect long-term benefits — primarily repeat business from guests participating in the event.

Too often restaurants are willing to pile up promotional costs on the front end with little or no idea if they'll turn a profit. **Optimism is no substitute for intelligent planning.**

Backtime

Speaking of planning, the best course of action is to "backtime" the essentials of the promotion. Working in reverse, day by day, plan all of the steps needed to execute the event. You may discover that time constraints prohibit you from doing everything you originally wanted to do. The idea is to spot trouble before you've dug in your heels.

As you backtime each day of the promotion, detail only the task, the person responsible for completing the task and the time by which the task should be completed. It's a tough but rewarding job that forces you to think through each detail of what needs to be done.

Don't forget about including incentives, contests and rewards, either. Used in concert with the promotion, they can fuel enthusiasm while keeping promotional elements top-of-mind with employees and guests alike.

Guarantee message

It begins with a button or sticker on the employee or a table tent. Guests become managers — they watch employees' performance when the manager cannot. When visiting a convenience store with a sign above the register, "If you fail to get a receipt, your purchase is free," what is the guest thinking? "Please forget, please forget, please forget." The employee knows the guest is watching and provides the receipt. Of course, the real reason the sign is there is so the cashier enters the sales into the register, but those thoughts aren't going through the guests' minds — they want something free!

By using a guarantee message in the restaurant, managers can get what they want, whether it's suggestions, sales entered properly or mentioning promotional items. Guests, meanwhile, have a little fun trying to catch employees making a mistake.

Some ideal guarantee messages could be:

○ If the cashier fails to suggest _____, the guest receives a free meal.

○ If the time at the drive-thru window is more than _____ seconds, the meal is free.

○ If the actual delivery time versus the quoted time is more than 10 minutes off, receive a free appetizer on your next order!

The beauty of this approach is that the system manages employees when nobody is around. Leverage the impact by training employees properly and make sure these types of suggestions aren't going on:

○ "I have to suggest the larger value meals or you get it free, so would you like one?"

○ "If I don't ask, I get in trouble, so would you like the two-fer pizza special?"

○ "Here are the desserts (pointing to the menu). We have to show it. You don't want anything do you?"

This approach ensures compliance. True excellence focuses on a system where a leader is always present to lead the employee through *Quick Service That Sells!*

Worse yet, poor employees might purposely not suggest the item so the restaurant has to provide it for free. Those employees need to work elsewhere! The chapter on "situational selling" provides many effective suggestions. Combining an incentive program with situational sales training and a guarantee message will ensure incredible results.

Other promotions

After you've lassoed new business and simultaneously trained your crew to maximize its service and sales potential during the promotion, consider using bouncebacks to generate repeat traffic. Bouncebacks are promotional offerings that are good the *next* time guests come in. Make them compelling and create a sense of urgency to redeem by making them good for only a short time.

Charity events

Have an evening when a percentage of sales is donated to a local charity. Contact the press to cover the event. Guests will be encouraged to try the restaurant and public relations will help build word-of-mouth. You may even get an article in the paper from the reporter who experienced the new level of service.

VIG card

To reward regulars and build loyalty, create a "very important guest" card. Whether it offers a progressive discount or a reward (spend $100 and receive a $10 gift certificate), guests will be more likely to return. The card also signals that the guest is a regular! If possible, use the POS system to track the promotion.

Loyalty programs tend to work better than discounts because guests feel more bonded to the brand and it doesn't cheapen the image of the restaurant like discounts tend to do. Airlines have perfected the system with their frequent fliers. Take a page from their book and modify it to work in your restaurant.

Fund-raisers

Invite schools or community groups in on various evenings and donate a part of the proceeds to their cause. Most restaurants need weekday business. Set up a system with the 20 or so schools around you and assign each a specific day of the month (Monday–Thursday over four weeks). Donate 5 percent of the sales. It's an effective way to stay involved in the community and encourage visits from guests who haven't come in for a while.

Sales bingo

Provide guests with a punch card to try a variety of different items. Once a row on the card is completed, they receive a prize and recognition. You can try it to encourage guests to order appetizers, desserts, a variety of specials, or a string of lunch visits during the business week.

Local offices and churches

Have they sworn off the place because of inadequate service in the past? Send them an invitation, including an incentive or time guarantee, to "give us another try." Better yet, personally visit them. Ask if the employees of the business eat at the restaurant frequently. If not, find out why and fix it! Become involved and build your brand — the workers in the immediate area will become high-frequency users.

Database

If you have the ability to track purchases by consumer, sort the information and invite back those guests who haven't been in for a while. On the flip side, find those who have spent the most money and send them a thank-you gift or free meal for their loyalty.

Build a buzz

Do unique things such as trivia while you wait, every 100th guest is free, random desserts or appetizers on the house, etc. Advertising is expensive. Buzz is free and attracts attention: "You have to go to _____. They do_____."

There are plenty of great marketing books to provide ideas to attract guests to the restaurant (Call Pencom International at 800-247-8514 or visit www.pencominternational.com). None is stronger than word-of-mouth. Implementing the ideas in this book will create a magnet, pulling guests in again and again to experience *Quick Service That Sells!*

chapter fifteen

Action Plan

It's nearly time to get on the floor and begin delivering **Quick Service That Sells!** Is the crew ready? Are the managers ready? Review these items, then see what a restaurant experience looks like when the service sizzles and you can step back and say *Now That's* **Quick Service That Sells!**

Quick Service That Sells! Implementation Checklist

Phase I

- Meet with managers to discuss leading the **Quick Service That Sells!** revolution.
- Conduct employee focus group to gather service suggestions and recommendations.
- Select three to four key employees (cashiers, phone reps, drive-thru) and train them to deliver **Quick Service That Sells!**
- Identify gaps and main priorities for the next 30 days (you can list all the gaps, but focus on only three or four main items initially).
- Conduct crew rally:
    - Describe the "perfect visit" for employees so they can visualize it.
    - Have managers role play "service" vs. **Quick Service That Sells!**
    - Review sizzle points with crew members.
    - Train crew on hospitality and how to say things to guests.
    - Cover situational selling with cashiers and validate them.

- Have "test employees" discuss how easy it is, the difference it makes and how much more lucrative it is (through incentives).
- Have guests discuss how much better the new service is.

○ Focus on the "fork" — regular or first-timer?

○ Manage the sizzle, conduct daily shift meetings focused on hospitality; provide constant communication and feedback for crew.

○ Talk to guests to get their feedback.

○ Managers model the behaviors and constantly talk hospitality.

Now That's Quick Service That Sells!

Phase II

○ Review Phase I — any modifications necessary?

○ Identify next set of priorities.

○ Work on honing in on customizing the experience (value-driven guests, celebrations, families, carryout, etc.).

○ Design sales and service contests to reward progress and encourage sales-building.

○ Make necessary adjustments.

○ Spread the word in the community — it's time for the neighborhood to get "experienced."

○ Dominate the competition!

Now That's Quick Service That Sells!

Restaurant managers' jobs are to provide outstanding guest experiences to make the competition suffer. Competitors, meanwhile, can try to copy the concept, menu and service. As they spend time trying to replicate it, move on to the next level. Always stay one step ahead. You're armed with the secret weapons — the passion to deliver **Quick Service That Sells!** and the ability to reward, recognize and constantly develop the team that provides it — something competitors cannot copy.

Oh, they can hope they can take care of guests adequately, but **Quick Service That Sells!** managers and crew *expect* to deliver service excellence to every guest, every visit. Those managers are conductors and employees the orchestra creating a sizzling experience ....

As I entered the restaurant, the crew greeted me.

Crew: "Welcome to _____!"

Cashier: "You look really familiar — have you been here before?"

Me: "No, this is my first visit."

Cashier: "We specialize in service and great food! You can't leave here without trying the _____ . We are famous for it!"

Me: "Sounds great!"

Cashier: "The meal comes in two sizes. Our most popular is the large size or you can save 50 cents and get the smaller size. Which would you prefer?"

Me:	"The larger meal will be fine."
Cashier:	"Great! Your total is $5.97. May I have your name please?"
Me:	"Sheer"
Cashier:	"Thanks, Mr. Sheer. We will call you when your food is ready. In the meantime, help yourself to the beverage and condiment bar. Thanks!"
Expediter:	"Sheer — your hot delicious _____ meal is now ready!"
Me:	"Looks great!"
Expediter:	"My name is John. Feel free to let me know if you need anything else."

I sat down and was enjoying some great food as well as seeing the crew out interacting and assisting guests. Certainly is reassuring to see things better than they have to be versus "good enough."

As I was finishing up my meal, the manager stopped by.

Manager:	"Thanks for visiting us tonight. I understand it's your first time here. How's the food and service? My name is Jim, and you are?"
Me:	"TJ, and it has been outstanding."
Manager:	"Glad to hear that. How did you hear about us?"
Me:	"I'm in town for a few days for a conference and some friends told me about it."

Manager: "If you'd like to come back tomorrow, here's a coupon for a free dessert. Hope you can make it."

Me: "Thanks!"

Now That's Quick Service That Sells!

APPENDIX A

*Now **That's*** Quick Service That Sells!
Crew Training Handout

*(For a free downloadable file of this handout,
visit www.pencominternational.com)*

Sample Questions:

1. For here or to-go?

_____

2. Decided yet?

_____

3. Is that all? Anything else?

_____

4. No problem.

_____

5. No.

_____

6. a. Can I get you an order of _____?

_____

  b. Would you like an appetizer [or desserts, etc]?

_____

  c. You don't want _____ do you?

_____

7. Small, medium or large?

_____

Sample Answers:

1. Welcome! Today we are featuring ....

2. Our most popular item is/The best deal is.

3. May I make a few suggestions?

4. My pleasure/I'd be happy to ....

5.   a. What I can do is ....

    b. The best way to do that is...

6. Today we are featuring _____ and _____, which would you prefer?

7. a. The large size is only _____ more

   b. We have two sizes of value meals. The most popular size is $_____ or you can save $_____ and choose the other one.

APPENDIX B

*Now **That's*** Quick Service That Sells!
Sizzle Points Handout (QSR)

*(For a free downloadable file of this handout,
visit www.pencominternational.com)*

Cashier *(and drive-thru if applicable)*

Friendly Greeting. Avoid 'here or to-go' or 'may I take your order?'

Situational Selling. Greet the guest and complete the order — what is missing that would enhance their meal?

Value meals. Offer a choice of two or more, not 'would you like to upsize.'

Maintain eye contact.

Explain the service sequence if the guest is new.

Food Delivery

Describe food using 'sizzle' words.

Confirm the order to the guest.

Thank and invite the guest back
('Next time don't forget to try the...').

Check back on the meal.

Offer a drink refill.

Facility

Restrooms

Windows

Beverage/Condiment bar

Floors

Exterior

Now That's Quick Service That Sells!
Sizzle Points Handout (QSR)
(continued)

The Guest Says/Does ...

What would you say?

1. Approaches the register.

_____

2. Asks: "What's the best deal?"

_____

3. Orders a _____.

_____

4. Orders a value meal.

_____

5. Says: "I've never been here before."

_____

6. Says: "I'll have a soft drink."

_____

7. Looks at the menu for a while.

_____

8. Pays and is about to walk away from the register.

_____

sizzle

SIZZLE POINTS

What would you say?

9. Food delivery to guest.

10. Table check back.

11. Guest leaving.

*Now **That's** Quick Service That Sells!*
Sizzle Points Handout (Pizza)

CSR/Phone Representative

Friendly Greeting. Avoid 'dine in or carry-out' or 'may I take your order?'.

Smile!

How many are they ordering for? **Suggest appropriate specials.**

Situational Selling. Greet the guest and complete the order — what is missing that would enhance the meal?

Value meals. 'You can get two pizzas for $_____ or save $_____ and only get one.

Quote accurate delivery time.

Carry-Out	Delivery
Describe food using 'sizzle' words.	Use names.
Confirm the order with the guest.	Thank and invite the guest back.
Offer a beverage while waiting.	Remind them to use the coupon next week.

The Guest Says/Does

What would you say?

1. Calls in

   _____

2. Asks 'What's the best deal?'

   _____

3. Orders a _____.

   _____

4. Orders one pizza

   _____

5. I've never been here before

   _____

6. Didn't order an appetizer

   _____

7. Didn't order dessert

   _____

8. Is a very large order (i.e. a kid's sleep-over)

   _____

SIZZLE POINTS

What would you say?

9. Waiting for their carry-out order

10. Carry-out pickup

11. Driver doing a delivery

APPENDIX C

The Pulse Check Card

(For a free downloadable file of this handout,
visit www.pencominternational.com)

(QSR)

1. Open the door and welcome any arriving guests and thank departing guests.

2. Ring up orders.

3. Make an order in the kitchen.

4. Take a drive-thru order.

5. Food delivery to guest.

6. Go to the restroom *(and send someone of the opposite sex into the other one!)*.

7. Check back on a guest.

8. Check the beverage or condiment bar *(if applicable)*.

9. Take a 'cleanliness' lap around the building.

10. Run a sales and product mix report.

11. Recognize an employee!

(Pizza)

1. Open the door and welcome any arriving guests and thank departing guests.

2. Answer the phone and take an order.

3. Make an order in the kitchen.

4. Food delivery to a carry-out guest.

6. Go to the restroom *(and send someone of the opposite sex into the other one!)*.

7. Call back a guest who ordered yesterday.

8. Take a 'cleanliness' lap around the building.

9. Run a sales and product mix report.

10. Recognize an employee!

APPENDIX D

Word Association

*(For a free downloadable file of this handout,
visit www.pencominternational.com)*

Here are a few things commonly thought of when hearing the featured words. Ask employees if any of these were on their list.

Run

> Jog, exercise, fast, slow, sweat, work-out, walk (or anything to do with exercise), copies, for office, shift/food/restaurant, election, panty-hose, stockings, on a bank, DMC, Forrest Run, river/creek/water, food, a shift, a restaurant

Sell/Cell

> Buy, price, deal, phone, amoeba, biology, division, auction, online, trade-in, financing, deal, battery,

Sale/Sail

> Price, cheap, deal, garage, boat, wind, mast, catamaran, away

Buy/By/Bi-

> Purchase, price, trade, book/author, two (i.e. bicycle), one get one free, sexual,

Strike

> Bowling, 10 pins, X, stop work, union, ball, baseball, three and you're out, fired, match, punch, hit, blow, lucky (cigarette brand), picket

Fall

Trip, cool weather, tree, hurt, September, October, November, tumble, take the blame, leaves,

Set

Dry, cement, glue, harden, tennis/game/match, inflexible, won't change, group of items, taken care of (all set), volleyball

Fair/Fare

Toll, cost to ride, taxi, bus, rides, amusement, games, equal, proportionate, treatment, OK, medical condition, weather

More Products and Services from Pencom International

Service That Sells!®

Quick Service That Sells!® **video.** Speed, accuracy, service and sales — improve it all with this self-paced program produced specifically for the QSR industry. Send a consistent message to your staff and teach them specific ways to enhance the guest dining experience. Available in English (TVC-76) or Spanish (TVC-76S) versions. 9 min. $99

Quick Service That Sells!® **book.** Speed, accuracy, quality, value, consistency, service, atmosphere and personalization — dramatically improve in each of these critical areas with this best-seller written specifically for the QSR industry. Teach your staff quick-service skills to build sales and increase repeat customers. (PUB-512P) $19.95

Work Smarter, Not Harder! the Service That Sells! Workbook for Quickservice. The Quick *Service That Sells!*® philosophy is incorporated into *Work Smarter, Not Harder!* strategies for QSR employees. These techniques will improve crew performance by pinpointing speed, accuracy, quality, value, consistency, service, atmosphere and personalization. (PUB-552) $4.95 each. Minimum order of 10 required.

©2004 Pencom International • 800.247.8514

PencomOnline.com

You can provide your employees with information. Or you can train them.

(Which do you think will work best?)

PencomOnline.com is an online portal that hosts interactive, real world training to meet your individual needs. With this flexible tool, your team members can set their own pace ... and you can simplify the training process. It's a convenient alternative to traditional "classroom" training ... and it's just as effective. (In fact, because of your computer-savvy, tech-hungry employees, it may be even more effective.)

The Power of the Web. (And why it matters to you.)

The web allows us to create flexible, interactive training that fully engages learners with animation, a high level of interactivity, multi-media simulations, role-play opportunities and audio narration. And, the web also allows you to eliminate manuals and hand grading tests as well as ....

- Train every employee with the same information regardless of unit location (anywhere in the world!)
- Easily keep materials current
- Provide specialized training from leading experts in the industry
- Utilize 24-hour, seven-day-a-week professional technical and instructor support
- Receive trainee test scores and reports in seconds online and via e-mail through any Internet connection using your secure name and password.

Two Options for More Flexibility...

I. Enjoy Corporate Billing and Customized Portals
Create the program that works best for you. If you're a multi-unit establishment, PencomOnline.com can provide you with a corporate billing account and customized portals and tracking systems. Then you can deliver all of our featured courses to employees and managers anywhere in the world. We provide flexible corporate billing, pre-payment or pay-per-use transaction models ... and group rates can be applied to all courses based on your number of units and estimated usage.

2. Create a Custom Virtual University (with little or no upfront cost!)

We'll create your own university for your 15+ multi-unit operation with a per-head or per-unit-flat rate (monthly, quarterly or annual subscription). How that university looks is up to you! We can ....

- Convert your existing training to online courseware
- Mix and match custom material with our standard courseware to develop your own curriculum
- Generate chain, regional, unit and trainee reports
- Design individual curriculum for each position
- Create a communication center with e-mail links and private message boards
- Rollout just-in-time training for new menu items or system-wide promotions

The Cost-Effectiveness of the Web. (And how you can save.) With PencomOnline.com, you'll eliminate costly training time... and you'll stop spending the thousands it takes to train each employee and grade tests. You'll also find that you may already have what you need...

- Designed for 56K dialup connection
- No special software needed
- Touch screen compatible
- Train on any computer with an Internet connection and Microsoft® Internet Explorer

With several pay-per-use payment options — credit card, online check and monthly corporate billing — you'll find PencomOnline is even more cost-effective ... call **800.247.8514** or visit us online at **www.pencominternational.com** for more information.

Workshops

Interaction, motivation and education are all part of Pencom International's keynote addresses and participant centered workshops. Each presentation is tailored to fit the specific needs of the group — engaging audiences from the start. Thousands of trainers, managers and staff have been motivated to increase workplace productivity by attending Pencom International's riveting workshops and keynotes. Audiences will walk away with relevant ideas and feasible action plans.

Workshops Offerings (facilitated in 2-4 hour sessions)

Service That Sells!®️ workshop. Management and staff will learn practical ideas to increase sales, improve service and encourage repeat business — the sky's the limit when you learn to execute these secrets to hospitality excellence and profitability (for management or staff).

Slam Dunk Marketing workshop. Step by step, you'll learn to maximize profits while minimizing expense during this in-house marketing revelation (for management).

Staff Up! workshop. Refine your existing skills and learn new ones in the art of recruiting, interviewing and retaining an all-star team (for management).

Handbooks

The Real World Management Series Handbooks. There's no time to waste on training that doesn't get results in the *Real World.* Read these life-changing handbooks in just **one** hour. Learn pinpoint strategies that will maximize your time and bring more happiness into your life. $12.95 each

Get a Life. Running your restaurant without running out of time. Do you eat, sleep and breathe your restaurant? If so, *Get a Life* today. This handbook will teach you the art of delegation and organization to manage your time without losing control. (PUB-600) $12.95

Staff Up! Assembling a team that sticks and clicks. Behind every good manager is a great staff. Learn how to create a winning team that sticks around. (PUB-601) $12.95.

Leadership now. Achieving restaurant management excellence in 30 days. Lead your staff with confidence! These concrete strategies will guide you through the leadership process. (PUB-602) $12.95

No Train? No Gain! Developing and delivering a training program that gets results. Take the training challenge and reap the rewards. Examine your training program from start to finish and discover strategies to improve current training as well as ingenious ways to create new ones. (PUB-603) $12.95

Books

The 52 Ways Series Books. Proven ideas for every week of the year. Put an end to turnover. Build a reliable staff. Pump up your profits. It's all here in this innovative series.

Turn the Tables on Turnover: 52 Ways To Find, Hire and Keep the Best Hospitality Employees book. An essential staff-management tool with tips on recruiting, interviewing, hiring and managing for retention. (PUB-523) $19.95

All for One: 52 Ways To Build a Winning Team book. Promote the brand equity of your operation and empower your staff. (PUB-543) $19.95

Playing Games at Work: 52 Best Incentives, Contests and Rewards for the Hospitality Industry book. The ultimate guide for stimulating staff motivation and improving performance in the areas of sales, customer service, waste watching and product knowledge. (PUB-520) $19.95

Pump Up Your Profits: 52 Cost-Saving Ideas To Build Your Bottom Line book. Timeless measures to widen your profit margin and narrow wasteful practices. (PUB-541) $19.95

Pour It On: 52 Ways To Maximize Your Bar Profits book. An invaluable behind-the-bar resource. (PUB-540) $19.95

Send Flowers to the Living book. From author TJ Schier ... learn how to build sales, profits and retention through employee loyalty in your business. Similar to a 'frequent-flier' approach used by the airlines — managers, leaders and owners will see how to create a system that rewards the 'frequent-performers.' The book is filled with many easy-to-implement ideas that can be used immediately!

Learn how to:

- Create a recognition culture
- Tie incentive programs to business goals
- Reward top performers
- Design effective contests with limited downside risk

(PUB-557) $16.95

To order, call 800.247.8514 or visit www.pencominternational.com